Everybody
Has A Tumor

Everybody Has A Tumor

Cures for the negative thoughts that are cancerous to our lives

Brian R. King

Everybody Has A Tumor
Cures for the negative thoughts that are cancerous to our lives

This Book Is Published by Change Your Life, Inc.
And Is Available Only At
www.BrianRKing.com

ISBN: 0-595-16735-7

Printed in the United States of America

This book is dedicated to my friends.
Those I have known, those I have now,
those I have just met, and those I have yet to meet.
May your lives be based in peace, love and hope
and filled with one success after another.

THANKS IS OWED TO:

Jack Canfield

He is without question the finest human being I've ever worked with and has taught me more about embracing my humanity than any 1,000 people I've met.

Amanda Reid, MSW

Without her encouraging me to take my ideas out of my head and put them on paper, this book may have never been written.

Dr. Kimberly Mann, DSW

She is not only the poster child for how to be absolutely brilliant and remain humble at the same time, but she is also the quintessential model of compassion, objectivity and what it means to give of yourself to others.

Michael Scott Karpovich, CSP

The title for this book was his idea.

Special Thanks to:

Marianne King (my mother and biggest fan) There are no words to describe the value her support has brought to my life.

Virginia Zahaitis (4th Grade Teacher) for always encouraging me to think positively when everything else around me was negative and making positivity so accessible in her presence.

Beverly Hajjar (5th Grade Play Director) she allowed me to be creative and encouraged as well as guided me to give nothing less than what I was capable of giving. She always made me feel that who I was was the best thing I could offer people.

Molly Gallagher (6th Grade Teacher) she treated my first efforts at writing like Pulitzer Prize winning material, which accelerated my passion for writing.

Barbara Clark (7th Grade Social Worker) for her unconditional support and guidance. She had an ability to help me feel powerful and confident when those around me were determined to take those feelings away.

Gail Aronoff (11th-12th Grade Teacher to the present) she always encouraged me to reach my highest potential of creativity, and when I reached it she encouraged me to go even higher. She continues to be a positive force as I continue on my path in life.

Don Zabelin (11th Grade Teacher) for his sense of humor and ability to be childlike and professional at the same time. He has a warm, optimistic spirit, which he saw and encouraged in me as well.

Ann Fagerland (12th Grade Teacher) she was the first English teacher I had that encouraged me to find my own voice in my writing. She supported my voice without judgment. It was during this time that I developed the ability to express myself with the written word, a skill that became indispensable when dealing with the most difficult time of my life.

Betty C. Andrews (12ᵗʰ Grade Teacher) She believed without a doubt that she would see me one day with my name in lights.

Katherine King (my wife) Every time I set a goal for myself she continues to offer her unconditional support no matter what the risk. For no other reason than that she believes in me.

I hope everybody who is reading this book has read this part first. This is one point that must be understood. Of the thousands of people I've come across in my life, it was the people above that supported me consistently and unconditionally. They each appeared in my life during a time when it seemed no one was on my side. It is often a single phrase, like Betty Andrews' prediction, that sends your thinking and your life into a totally new and rewarding direction. The biggest lesson to be learned from them and others like them is that people will line up to discourage you, but when those that will support you show up, it makes all of the difference in the world.

Finding those special people in life is like panning for gold: you may spend years finding nothing more than dirt and rock, but one day you find the golden nugget you've been looking for making the entire journey worthwhile. But when you find someone who believes in you, trust that belief unconditionally because what they see in you stems from the best parts of life: hopes, dreams, determination, good-will, unselfishness, compassion and honesty etc.

Discouragement stems from those things that keep us from succeeding: fear, doubt, disbelief, and anything else that compels us to seek safety in limited thinking instead of venturing out and taking the risks that lead to growth. It's the believers and risk takers who've made the world what it is. When they throw some of that belief your way, grab it; hold on tight and ride it until it appears in your life the way it appears in your mind and in their hearts.

We all have dreams, but until we take action to realize them, we have no chance of living the life our heart and mind have showed us is right for us. So dream, dare, act and live fully.

CONTENTS

INTRODUCTION

An intricate universal web binds all of life together. Each strand connecting one life to all others, as such a movement on one strand creates movements on the others as well. This fact is best demonstrated in a concept referred to as the "butterfly factor." Simply put, the butterfly factor states that since all of life is inextricably interconnected, if a butterfly in the Central United States suddenly flaps its wings, you will see rain fall in New York where clear skies were previously predicted. I can't tell you how many times I've seen a weatherman slapped in the face with his own confidence when some unforeseeable force came out of no where and turned his beloved forecast on its head.

I don't mention this in order to offer a new process for weather prediction. I offer this to you because of a very important life principle that it embodies, which is that even the slightest action can create profound change. It then stands to reason that when more action is taken, then even greater change can take place.

History is filled with evidence of the profound change that came from a single action. Think of the change that came about with the uttering of such phrases as, "Let my people go," or "I have a dream." Think of how one man's single decision to become a doctor led to the cure for polio. Even more simply than that, how powerful the phrase "I love you" can be to someone whose day was changed for the better after hearing it.

Profound change often begins with single actions, which include decisions. In this book I will recommend many actions that can be taken to create profound change in your life beginning immediately.

When each of us is conceived into and nourished by our mother's womb, we are as a chrysalis. Undergoing profound transformation with growth as the only objective. Then during a miraculous process we break out of that world into a brand new life, a new freedom with unlimited possibilities.

Most of us, however, slowly begin to wrap ourselves up in a new cocoon. As we are introduced to one limiting belief after another, we often choose to believe and accept these limitations, a straightjacket of our own creation. We often end up going through life being guided by more rules that hold us back than set us free. It is time to break out.

As with birth and as with the emerging of the monarch butterfly from its cocoon, there comes a point when we receive the signal to shed the straightjacket that is the only thing remaining between us and a new life. This signal, or **inspiration for transformation**, compels us to rediscover and recover the unlimited world we once knew. Time to begin.

I use the metaphor of the butterfly to illustrate where it is we're going. But next I discuss a metaphor that best describes what keeps us from getting there. As we begin our journey in this book, I will be discussing at great length my personal battle with a physical cancer. This book is not about physical cancer as such, it is about the psychological and emotional cancers that are nurtured and grow daily by our choosing. These are the cancers I was forced to confront as a result of my physical cancer.

The limiting beliefs and thinking that we indulge in that rob us of the positive, life-affirming energy needed for growth have the same detrimental effects as a tumor. These thoughts take the energy from positive areas of your life and then grow and grow, leaving only destruction in their wake. The only way to stop this process is to find a cure. You must take the energy away from the tumors so they can no longer grow and will weaken, shrink, disappear and never return. This book offers such cures for the self-imposed cancerous thinking that hold us back.

This book is about the process of transformation I went through, from a life filled with self-imposed limitations to one that is limitless. It is about the cure for my physical cancer but more important for my psychological and emotional cancers. The physical cancer was the major turning point in my life—my **inspiration for transformation.** The difficulty I had in dealing with the problems that arose from the circumstances having cancer put me in compelled me to change the way I thought about and thus lived my life. It is these problems that you need to focus on while reading my story. Concentrate on the transformation.

Those who've reached the point in their lives where a significant change is necessary are inspired to transform for many reasons: bankruptcy, divorce, death of a loved one or any other event that serves as an inspiration for transformation. If this is something you face, as you read my story, allow yourself to see what is inspiring your change. Once identified, you will be better able to embrace the techniques that help transformation into an unlimited life possible.

By practicing and implementing the techniques that I learned through my own experience in overcoming adversity, I discovered the cures for what ailed me. I was able to achieve a greater sense of mastery in my everyday life. I believe they can have the same benefit for you. The cancer experience was the furnace that forged the person I am today. As I tell my story I use as much detail as possible to provide you with the experience of being right along side me as I endure the various struggles before me. My experiences were intense and overwhelming, and yet they were survivable and life was even better when they were resolved. If I can survive struggles of this magnitude, I can survive anything, and so can you.

When I finally sat down to write this book, it was mainly at the behest of my colleagues who encouraged me to put my ideas on paper. I've always been told that I have a way of taking difficult concepts or problems and simplifying them, especially the problems of everyday

xviii   Everybody Has A Tumor

life. I am grateful that I am able to do this, but bear in mind it isn't a special ability, it is an acquired skill that I learned because I was caught up in a situation with no other practical way of viewing things.

As I've gotten to know people over the years since my illness, they would often bring up problems they were having in their own lives and I would offer them a metaphor that I believed might help illuminate their situation. Their attitudes would quickly change, and they would ask where I'd heard the advice I'd just given them. When I told them I had just thought it up they looked pleasantly surprised and asked if I would write it down for them.

It wasn't before long that I had a stack of papers that composed the heart of my life philosophy. But it wasn't until I encountered one colleague in particular that my ideas came together in the form you have before you. One day while having lunch in between classes during my senior year in college, I overheard some of my classmates discussing their stress over upcoming midterm exams. They began tossing around ideas about how to deal with the stress. They asked me how I dealt with it, and I told them, that I don't get test anxiety.

They were shocked and asked, "How the heck I was able to do that?"

I began a simple explanation about striving for control where I had it and leaving the uncertainty of the test experience to its own devices. Again I was asked where I received that advice. To which I responded, "It's just how I think."

I was asked by one of them if I'd written it down someplace? To which I responded, "No, why?"

I'd never considered that things I normally just did would be of any significant value to others. It was then that one of them, a girl named Amanda, went into a lengthy explanation as to why what I had just said would be of great value to her and potentially others.

I found her comments and confidence in my ideas very empowering. I consequently went home and began expanding on our conversation. Before I knew it I had thirty pages worth of ideas. What started out as a simple response to Amanda's request has now become a guide for transforming your life. I regularly slobber all over her with gratitude for her encouragement. It just goes to show that one person's belief in another can go a long way. Hopefully, my belief in you will flow from this book and into your life.

One final note before we begin. Many people who've taken the risk to dramatically change their lives have done so in response to a powerful inspiration for transformation, or not so powerful. It is basically something that made change more desirable and more necessary than complacency. The better you understand your inspiration, the easier it will be to begin. The caterpillar is able to transform into a butterfly because it understands itself as a caterpillar. But keep in mind that you don't need to know absolutely everything about yourself at the outset, if you did you wouldn't need to read this book. So be prepared to uncover things you didn't know were there. Even in a caterpillar's transformation there are things that take care of themselves by virtue of going through the process, but you will become aware that they are changing and you must commit to the process. Are you ready for a cure? Then it's time to begin.

PART ONE:

FROM DARKNESS TO LIGHT

Doubt closes your eyes and
darkens them to the possibilities.
Hope opens them up again.

CHAPTER ONE

My Story of Adversity

I was eighteen years old when I was thrust into a period of chaos that I never could have imagined. Over the course of that year my life nearly disintegrated and thus needed to begin again in a whole new way. That year was the defining point in my life. During it I was forced to reexamine who I had been, who I had become and who I needed to be. This is my story of adversity.

The Journey Begins

All of my life I never thought anything really bad would happen to me. As long as I prayed, confessed my sins and led a good life, I believed all the bad things would befall the next guy. I never would have guessed that I would become the next guy.

It all began in the middle of my eighteenth year. I was a senior in high school at the time. I was lying in bed one night, trying to fall asleep, when a sharp pain shot into my abdomen. It felt as if I had just been kicked in the groin. The pain was so excruciating that I doubled over and shouted a popular four-letter word, and it wasn't "FORK!" The pain felt like it started in my right testicle. When I checked it I found that there was a very tender lump near the top of the testicle. I knew my body well enough to know that this was something new and didn't belong there. I felt I should have it looked at.

As Murphy's Law dictates, this problem dealt with a part of my anatomy that I wasn't comfortable discussing openly. However, urgent need for action superceded my fear of embarrassment, so I walked upstairs to my parents bedroom. When given permission to enter, I spoke quickly to facilitate a fast exit. I told my mother that I had a bump on my right testicle and it hurt really badly. I further stated I thought it would be a good idea to see the doctor. She looked at me, somewhat surprised, and simply said, "Okay." I suspect there isn't a passage in the parents handbook for how to respond to the statement I had just made. I closed their bedroom door and went back to my room. As I lay in bed I tried to relax and kept thinking to myself,

"It's nothing, it's nothing." I was finally able to fall asleep.

Before I awoke the following morning, my mom had already made an appointment with our family physician, Dr. H. I didn't tell my siblings why I was going to the doctor because I felt a little strange and self-conscious about the nature of my problem. Once there I explained to the doctor what had happened the night before. She asked me a series of questions about the pain when it occurred to me that I had experienced periods of discomfort a month prior. I experienced an achy feeling in my groin that would last a day or two, all the time varying in intensity. I didn't notice any lump when I examined myself then, and the pain eventually went away. So I wrote it off as the typical growing pains of an 18-year-old male and forgot about it. It wasn't until this lump suddenly showed up with this excruciating pain that I felt compelled to have it checked out.

The doctor examined the lump. It was round and about the size of a pea. "Ouch!" I shouted as she pressed on it, causing pain to again shoot into my abdomen. The pain throbbed for a few minutes, and I began feeling a little sick to my stomach. The doctor said it felt like it might be a cyst, but, if it were it wasn't common for it to be so painful. She said she didn't want to take any chances, so she went to the phone and called a colleague of hers named Dr. N. who was a pediatric urologist. She told him what she had found and said, "I don't care who you have to bump off your schedule. You have to see this kid tomorrow."

I went home and spent the rest of the day feeling anxious and impatient. I was aware of the pain more than ever, which only made it worse. As stressful as having to wait until the next day for an answer to my problem was, what other choice did I have? The next day first thing in the morning I was in Dr. N's office.

He examined me as the previous doctor had and arrived at the same conclusions, which brought about the same concerns. He wanted to have an ultrasound exam of my right testicle performed to determine whether the lump was a cyst or not. Unfortunately, the local hospital where he was on staff had no openings for two weeks so I was forced to wait. I quietly began to develop fears of what the lump might be. Every time I had heard the term lump used in relation to a body part, it was inevitably followed by the word "cancer." I kept telling myself that if cancer was a possibility then the doctors wouldn't wait; they'd be concerned and want to act sooner. I continually went through the rationalizing cognitive song and dance of it couldn't happen to me anyway because these things only happen to other people. With this I did my best to squelch my fears because I didn't want to worry until there was something to worry about. So I kept my fingers crossed, rooted for a cyst and tended to my schoolwork and other life matters – all the while trying not to think about it. Easier said than done, especially because the lump was still pretty painful.

Occasionally the lump would begin to throb again, which made me inclined to check it each time (in private of course). As the days passed the lump felt like it was getting bigger. It gradually lost its smooth surface in favor of a bumpier more irregular one. As it got more uncomfortable and I got more anxious, I kept telling myself,

"It's nothing, it's nothing."

Nothing was the only thing I could handle it being. When the day of the ultrasound finally arrived, I asked my mother to go with me for support. If it turned out to be something, I didn't want to be alone when I found out. Fortunately my mother had already decided that nothing would keep her from being there with me.

Once there, I was taken to the examining room. Unexpectedly Dr. N. the urologist appeared. I had had a lot of tests in the past for various reasons, and this was the first time any doctor of mine had shown up for it. I didn't know if this was good or bad. He asked me how I was doing and I told him that I felt the lump was getting bigger.

He proceeded to examine my testicle again and observed that the lump seemed to have doubled in size since he had seen me two weeks earlier. The expression on his face didn't change, which to me meant he wasn't feeling any overwhelming concern at this development. I thought for an instant that maybe I was overreacting and this is just what cysts do. But then he turned to the technologist who was to perform the test and asked if she wouldn't mind if he had another doctor do the exam. He briefly left the room and returned with Dr. B. the head of the radiology department. He performed the exam as he and my doctor viewed the images on a small video monitor. They kept convincing poker faces as they pointed at the screen and made little comments about what they were seeing. Their demeanor led me to feel that nothing in what they were seeing was of any real concern.

At the completion of the exam, Dr. N. asked me to sit in the waiting room where he'd come talk to my mother and me in a few minutes. I remember telling my mom that it was probably nothing. Not much later Dr. N. came out and spoke to us. He told us that he had reviewed the films with the other doctor and that they had concluded that the lump in my testicle didn't appear to be a fluid filled cyst after all but, in fact, appeared to have a solid mass to it. Considering the fact that it was growing, it needed to be surgically removed as soon as possible. I felt my heart start racing as my thoughts of

"It's nothing" quickly changed to

"What is it?"

Again the word "cancer" started running through my head, but I didn't say anything. I really didn't know what to say. My mom asked if it could wait a few weeks because I would be graduating high school soon. Dr. N. said absolutely not, that it was imperative to get this taken care of immediately. We submitted, and he arranged for surgery to take place in two days.

During those couple of days I became very task oriented. I would be having surgery on a Wednesday and would have to remain in the hospital until Friday. I concerned myself with school and getting the assignments I would miss so I could work on them in the hospital. I studied whether I felt I needed to or not just to keep my mind occupied. I slept surprisingly well the night before the operation.

After I checked in with the receptionist, she took me to a dressing room. It would have been more appropriate to call it an undressing room because I had to remove all of my clothes and put this gown on that was open in the back so that all of my secrets could be revealed to the world. I hardly felt dressed at all.

When I was comfortably "dressed" in my oversized designer tissue, the receptionist sat me down with a lengthy release form to fill out before surgery. It asked for my permission for any of a list of things to take place during surgery. I became very nervous because I thought all of these things would take place if I signed it. Just then Dr. N. showed up. He would be performing the surgery and wanted to know if I had any questions. I told him I was concerned about the things I had just read. He told me that the items listed were only possibilities, not routine occurrences. The first thing I asked was if it was okay for me to cross out items that I wasn't willing to agree to, especially the part about the possibility that video cameras might be present in the operating room to film the procedure for educational purposes. The last thing I wanted was my crotch on PBS. He said it was perfectly all right to cross that out. He then sat down beside me, and we went through the form together.

He asked if I had any other questions, and there was only one on my mind:

"Are you going to have to take my testicle out?" He said he wouldn't know for sure until he saw what we were dealing with, but probably. I asked him to do his best to leave it intact. He then said he'd see me in a little while and left to prepare for surgery. I was then asked to lie down on a cart and was wheeled into a holding area where I was left to wait for a minute or two.

A young man walked in wearing a surgical cap and scrubs. He had a small bowl filled with soapy water in one hand and a small razor in the other. I could tell he sensed the awkwardness of the moment as he told me that it was his job to shave me before surgery. He wasn't referring to my face. He proceeded to lift the front of my scanty gown and go to work. We made very little eye contact as we engaged in light chit chat to get through the few minutes that it took, after which he covered me back up, wished me luck and left.

I was moved once again and briefly parked outside the door of the operating room where my surgery was to take place. A nurse came out with a syringe and said she had to give me a shot of a substance to make my mouth dry so I wouldn't be inclined to swallow and possibly vomit during surgery. That seemed very reasonable to me. Then the anesthesiologist came out and told me he was going to start an IV in my arm so he could administer the anesthesia. I turned my head away and could have sworn I heard a pop as I felt the sharp pain of the needle sliding into my arm. He told me when he was beginning to run the anesthesia and no sooner had he said that that I felt the lights go out.

Then next thing I remember was hearing a lady's voice calling my name as I fought to open my eyes. I finally managed to pry them open, and as they slowly came into focus, the first thing I saw was Dr. N's comforting face looking right at me. I later thanked him for that because there's nothing like coming out of a frightening experience and seeing a familiar face. I was still half sedated, but I mustered the strength to ask him in a groggy voice, "Is it gone?" Meaning did he remove my testicle. To this he nodded with a consoling look. "Oh no" I said while shaking my head. He patted me on the knee and said he would come up to my hospital room in about an hour to see me. He had made a good-size incision in my abdomen to remove the testicle and wanted me to stay a few days to make sure it was healing well before releasing me.

The Diagnosis

Dr. N. came to my room a while later where my mother and I were waiting. He asked how I was feeling, and I was feeling well, all things considered. Actually I was indulging in some hefty denial. I wasn't prepared to deal with the loss of my testicle. I viewed it as an assault upon my masculinity. As I gripped my mother's hand he told us he had been to the lab where my testicle had been sent for testing. Before he could say anything else my mother asked if it was cancer? He nodded and said, "Yes." I remember my stomach dropping and my mind going blank. "I'm dead" I thought to myself.

He went on to explain that it appeared the tumor had been growing for some time inside the testicle, which was why I had felt some discomfort over the past month. It wasn't until it got so large that it ran out of room and began to push against the wall of the testicle that it created a lump, which could be noticed. The reason it had hurt so much was that it was growing by the major blood supply to that testicle and was drawing so much blood that it began to hemorrhage. If it hadn't done that I may not have discovered the lump until it was too late. Talk about luck. He reassured us that he believed he had removed all of the cancerous cells but wanted me to come back in a month for a post-surgical blood test to confirm it.

Just like that my worst fear had been confirmed and relieved in almost an instant. Even though he had said he'd gotten it all, I had a hard time letting go of the news I'd just received. I had cancer. Even if it was gone, the fact that it had been there at all was terrifying. I still felt that I was diseased somehow and was afraid to feel relieved only to be hit with the news again. I wasn't sure what to do with myself. I didn't know whether to relax or panic. Either way I had a lot I would have to adjust to, and my life was obviously going to be quite different from this point.

It wasn't until later that night after my mom had left that I checked myself for the first time. It was a strange feeling to know that some part of my body had just been removed. But why did it have to be this part? I was an 18-year-old male and insecure enough about my manhood as it was. I was afraid to touch my scrotum because I didn't know if it would hurt or not. I gently palpated it and it actually felt normal—normal but partially empty. It felt so weird feeling only one testicle where there had previously been two. I really couldn't tell it was gone until I checked it. I thought it would be as noticeable as if I had lost a limb or something. Physically I couldn't sense that anything had changed. Mentally was another story.

I had been raised in a social environment where the male mentality was based on the superiority of their own equipment and making others feel insecure about their own via jokes and insults. (Which is of course *the best* reassurance a growing boy needs to foster his self-esteem!) However irrational this preoccupation might have been, it unfortunately was my only point of reference for forming my self-image. For this reason I began to feel inadequate—like part of my manhood had been taken away. Even worse was the embarrassment I felt every time a nurse would come into my room to check my incision. I knew how I'd learned to judge the virility of a man quantitatively speaking, and I was afraid these nurses judged according to the same criteria. I stopped counting the number of times I felt myself turning red.

I did my best not to deal with the loss at that time. Instead I tried to keep my mind focused on school by attempting to complete the work

I'd brought with me. With all the pain medication I was being given, math wasn't the easiest thing to do. I didn't get very much done. My mother came and stayed with me everyday. So when I wasn't struggling with geometry, her company provided more than a sufficient alternative to dealing with my insecurities. After three days I was allowed to go home. I was able to rest through the weekend before going back to school. I soon found out that I would not be returning to life as I knew it.

My Friends Receive the News

When I arrived at school the news of my diagnosis was already well circulated. My younger sister, who was also in high school at the time, and my girlfriend were openly voicing their concerns about my health to others. I was so self-conscious about my missing testicle that it was all I could think about. It was now common knowledge of where my cancer had been found and that I had been physically compromised. I subconsciously feared how others might judge me, and I consciously feared people lining up to stare at my crotch.

Not knowing how to deal with the immense insecurity I was feeling, I decided that I would just try and put it all behind me and attempt to get back to normal. It quickly became apparent that normal wasn't looking to get back to me. I began noticing a change in how my peers related to me. Except for a slight limp from the pain of my incision, outwardly I appeared unchanged. I had lost a testicle, which I would have to learn to deal with. Beyond that I didn't feel any different. I kept telling myself that as far as I was concerned, the cancer was gone and I had nothing to worry about, so I was going to continue as I had before.

My closest friends didn't treat me differently because they knew I was okay with everything. But others looked at me like they where surprised

I was still breathing. I kept getting questions like "Are you okay" or "Are you going to die?"

I was so shocked by the boldness of the question that I was tempted to say,

"I could go at any second, so you'd better back up so I don't land on you." Instead I replied, "I'm fine, the doctor thinks he got it all." "Good, good" they would say and then walk away.

What's wrong with these people I would wonder? The most shocking of all was how some of my "friends" stopped talking to me altogether. I couldn't understand why they had this reaction. I told them that I had had cancer, and upon hearing this, some of them just gave me a blank stare and walked away. What was up with that? What was the problem? I'm fine now. I decided that I just needed to blow them off because I had final exams and graduation to worry about. I would have to talk to them at another time.

The remaining few weeks of school were very difficult. I hadn't been able to study in the hospital because the morphine I was getting for pain made it difficult to concentrate. The painkillers I was given to take at home made me drowsy, and my final exam grades reflected that. I had gotten A's and B's until that point so I wasn't hurt that bad academically. I still wish I could have done better.

One Last Hurrah

Well, graduation came and went, and I was free to pursue my life. I began thinking once again as any 18 year old would. I was planning on a long, fun-filled summer, after which I would enroll in my local community college to begin studies in psychology. But before I could dive into the rest of my life, I had one last piece of high school business to take care of. I had been involved in my school's antidrug and alcohol clown troupe. We would put on makeup and funny clothes and travel to the area grade schools to perform original skits about the dangers of drug and alcohol use.

On July 4th I was celebrating my last hurrah with the troupe as we had been asked to participate in the Fourth of July parade for one of the surrounding communities. I remarked to one of my teammates, "I'd better enjoy this because this is probably going to be the last time I put on makeup." It turns out that my statement couldn't have been further from the truth.

During October of the previous year, I had auditioned for a school that I felt I had no hope of getting into, but I tried out anyway in response to peer and family encouragement. The audition was for acceptance into Ringling Brothers and Barnum and Bailey Clown College, which at the time was located in Venice, Florida. On the morning after the parade, my dad woke me up and said that Clown College was on the phone.

I jumped out of bed and quickly made my way to the kitchen. I picked up the phone and on the other end was Steve Smith, the dean of Clown College. He said that the reason he was calling was not only to inform me that I was accepted and to invite me to attend, but also to tell me that I had been accepted unanimously by the board of directors, which almost never happens. He asked if I would have any problems attending.

"Of course not" I told him and then thanked him profusely.

A chance to try out for "The Greatest Show on Earth." A chance to travel all over the country as a clown in a big top circus. I could barely contain myself.

For the past few weeks since graduation, I had been having problems with my wisdom teeth. I didn't want to have problems with them while I was away, so I had all four of them removed. They were all impacted so the doctor had to saw into my jaw to get them out. As a result, my mouth swelled shut and my face looked like a squirrel with a mouth full of nuts for the winter. I had two weeks to go before my flight, and it was now time for the follow-up blood test to my surgery. It was a simple procedure. I went to the hospital to have my blood drawn and went on my way.

Not So Fast

A few days later Dr. N. called and spoke to my mother. He said he wanted me to have another blood test, because he thought the lab might have made a mistake. When my mom asked why, he said the numbers in the resulting measurements seemed too high, and he wanted another test to make sure. When she told me, I thought nothing of it. So they made a mistake it happens. I had more blood drawn and went about my business. Another few days passed, and Dr. N. called back. I was out with my friends when my mother received the call.

He explained to her that before my surgery, blood was drawn to determine the levels of a certain protein in my blood, which is used to determine the presence of my type of cancer. Obviously, these numbers where high then. Immediately after surgery, more blood was taken that revealed that the level of that protein was normal and that cancer was no longer present. He was concerned when he received the results of the recent follow-up test because the numbers were three times higher than before surgery—which was why he suspected an error had been made. But he had just received my most recent test results, which were taken only a few days after the first test—and now the numbers where five times higher. He said there was no mistake—my cancer was back and growing quickly. He informed my mother that before he had called her, he had called several cancer centers all over the country to find out the best place to send me. The responses he got were unanimous, so I would be venturing to a hospital in Indiana. A doctor there was testing an experimental protocol on testicular cancer and was having great success with it. He told my mom to have me there in 24 hours to begin chemotherapy.

I got home late that night, and my parents decided to let me get a good night's sleep. In retrospect, I never did ask how well they slept that night. They came in my room together the next morning. I was still half asleep when they dropped the bomb. After taking a few seconds to comprehend what they'd said, I jumped out of bed and said, "Okay let's go get this over with." I was a little shocked by the news, but the problem had been remedied with such relative ease before that I thought it would only take a few days again. All I knew was I was leaving for Clown College in a week and had to get this out of the way. Mom said I was going to receive chemotherapy treatments. I had no idea what was in store for me. My mother was going to drive me to Indiana, so we spent the better part of the day packing for our trip. My father would have to stay behind to run the family business.

It took four hours to get there from our home in a Chicago suburb. I spent the trip looking at the scenery and spotting out-of-state license plates. Anything I could do except thinking about where we were going and what we were going for. I just wanted it over with already. We were fortunate enough to be able to reserve a room in a hotel across the street from the hospital. I was tired from the trip, so I was able to sleep relatively well that night. The next morning we had an early breakfast so I could be at the hospital by 7 a.m. as the doctor had requested. When it was about ten minutes until seven, we paid the waitress and walked across the street. I still really hadn't taken any of this seriously. I thought I'd get some medicine and go home.

Round One

We walked to the information desk, and my mother barely uttered my name to the woman sitting there, who quickly jumped from her seat and with a look of urgency said, "Oh yes we heard you were coming."

She called someone on the phone. Not a minute later a man flew around the corner with a wheelchair and whisked me away with my mother in tow. I was taken into a back room and asked to sit in a chair with an armrest that looked like one you'd find in a classroom. Two nurses were in there bouncing around the room, frantically getting supplies. At the time I thought they were in a hurry because they had other things to do. Then one of them came over and started an IV in my arm. I asked her what she was giving me. I was surprised when she told me it was the chemotherapy.

I didn't know what chemotherapy was. I didn't know it came in a plastic bag. Just as she was finishing, the door to the room opened and a small, thin gentleman wearing slacks and a dress shirt entered the room. There was a large entourage behind him. He introduced himself as Dr. E. and explained that he would be overseeing my treatment. He said the hospital had had a lot of success with my type of cancer, and he was confident that they could get rid of it for me. He then left, and two younger doctors from his group remained and began writing prescriptions for drugs to relieve various side effects of the chemotherapy.

With the chemo well underway, I was taken for a Cat Scan where I was made to drink two large cups of an iodine-based liquid dye mixed with fruit flavoring that might as well have been battery acid. The gag reflex it brought about in my throat was unrivaled in the history of modern nausea. I drank as much as I could, but it still wasn't enough for the exam, so they took me into the room and had me lie on the exam table where they injected a second dye into my arm to top off what I had drank. The subsequent exam revealed that my cancer had indeed spread and had formed a large tumor in one of my abdominal lymph nodes.

The roller coaster ride had begun with no sign of stopping anytime soon.

After several other tests, which lasted almost all day, I was finally taken up to my room. It wasn't until now that I was given the antinausea sedatives that where prescribed for me. They were powerful and hit me hard and fast. I became so loopy, for lack of a better word, that I started to forget where I was. I was attempting to relax after a horrible day when I quickly discovered what it meant to be a patient in a teaching hospital.

A medical student entered my room, whose infinite wisdom told him that my day just wouldn't be complete without a rectal exam—compliments of his index finger. After the day I'd had this was the straw that broke the camel's back. Through heavy sedation and a mouth still swollen shut from my dental surgery, it was difficult to express the humiliation this complete stranger was putting me through. This act of inconsideration made my stomach turn. My mother was watching me, and her instincts made her painfully aware of what was coming next. A nurse entered the room, saw the student in action and quickly kicked him out saying that it was a bad time. As he left the room, my mother rushed to my bedside with a washing basin as I proceeded to vomit everything I'd eaten since I was five years old. With a mouth that's swollen shut this was not an easy task. It was similar to what would happen if you placed your thumb partially over the end of a hose while water was coming out. Although I remember this event quite vividly, I believe it would have been much worse had I not been so medicated. After that I fell asleep from exhaustion.

The next day went a little better. I was still pretty out of it from the medication, so my mom took to answering all of the staff's questions on my behalf. I couldn't remember basic things, like my age or the day of the week. I mostly slept. I had my mom call my girlfriend so she could be brought up to date. She had no idea of the magnitude of the situation, as she seemed unconcerned as I described to her what was happening.

That night I started feeling pretty lousy. The medication finally had my nausea under control, but I started feeling a strong pressure in my chest. My heart started beating really fast and really hard. It beat so hard I could feel it pounding against the inside of my chest, and each beat was more painful than the last. It was beginning to get harder and harder to breathe. When my mom came back from getting something to eat, I told her how I was feeling. She asked the nurse to check me, and then I remember being moved to another room so I could be given oxygen. Either that night or early the next morning I was taken to have an echocardiogram, an ultrasound exam of the heart. It turned out that my heart was fine. The doctors believed I was just having palpitations as an adverse reaction to the chemotherapy drugs. Whatever the reason, that feeling was nasty—and frightening. If having the feeling that your heart was going to explode is typical of this treatment, I was terrified of what other pleasantries were on the horizon. By the middle of the next day, the symptoms had eventually subsided but left me even more exhausted.

The following morning my mother woke me and said she was going to the airport to pick up my father. Apparently she had spoken to him the night before, and he told her that he couldn't bear not being there with us. He would be leaving my older brother, Chris, in charge of the family business for the next couple of days. My 15-year-old sister, Melissa, would have to miss at least this week of her summer vacation, as she was put in charge of sitting at the desk and fielding phone calls.

Not long after my mother left, I was able to fall back to sleep. A while later I heard a voice asking me to wake up. My eyes sprung open to see a room full of people in white lab coats, with Dr. E. standing in the middle. What a rude awakening! This is Mr. King, Dr. E. told the group of whom I assumed were medical students. He briefly described the facts of my case to them, and they all turned and left the room without so much as a word to me. He'd spoken to them as though I were being presented as a diseased specimen and not a person.

I was very insulted by this intrusion. I wondered why he couldn't just let them peak in the room without waking me and then discuss me later. It was obvious they weren't interested in me as a person. Beyond meeting him my first day, this brief visit was the only time I saw him the entire week I was there. He was overseeing my treatment but knew nothing about me personally. I got the feeling that I was only a chart filled with symptoms and numbers to him. I was treated like a disease wrapped with a person, when what I really needed was to be treated like a person who happened to have a disease.

I learned that sleep for a patient in a hospital is a scarce commodity, because every time I started to get some, it was interrupted. Why does the staff insist on disturbing the few minutes of rest a patient is able to get? Sure, they had various tasks to accomplish, but it must have occurred to them at some point that lack of sleep might just be detrimental to the healing process. Alas, it didn't seem to matter to them. It might have helped if the doctor would have seen me and not just my chart. Maybe I could have asked him to allow me a little rest. In retrospect, though, I am able to put the feeling that I was disrespected aside. Dr. E. did develop the treatment I am receiving, so in light of this, any shortcomings I may have perceived in his care were miniscule.

One of the best memories I had of my stay there were the many visits I received from a nursing student named Honey. Yes, that was her real name. She would tell jokes, and do whatever it took to keep my spirits up. In spite of my condition she wouldn't tolerate my crabbiness. She would inflate latex gloves, draw smiley faces on them and hang them from my IV pole. I'll admit it was very difficult to be a grump with her around.

Another time during that week my uncle Lou and his wife, Kathy, drove down to the hospital from their home in Central Illinois to offer their support. I remember when they came into my room. Lou went to my father and shook his hand, while Kathy gave my mother a big hug. Kathy then walked over to my bed and touched my hand as she asked how I was doing. I was so sedated I don't even remember giving her an answer. I have always been grateful for their gracious gesture, and I thank them both every time I get a chance.

The hardest day of the week was Sunday. This was the day I was supposed to be boarding a plane for Clown College. Instead I was lying in a hospital bed hundreds of miles from home. While other kids my age were enjoying their summers and preparing for their futures, I was here fighting for my life, wondering if I would even have a future.

The next day I received the last of the chemotherapy for that week and began preparing to go home. One of my nurses briefed my mother and me on the course of my treatment from this point on. She told me that I would need a few more weeks of chemotherapy, but the doctor was going to arrange for another doctor at my local hospital to oversee my care. This meant I could finish my chemo near home. The nurse gave my mom information on my treatment and directions on taking care of me. She also gave my mom the name of the doctor who would be overseeing my treatment back home. I began feeling like I was being punished somehow. I felt cheated for not being able to go to Clown College and being forced to miss this tremendous opportunity, but I knew I clearly had bigger fish to fry.

I slowly staggered out of the hospital. My parents offered their help, but I wanted to walk by myself. I had been poked and prodded all week long. I wanted at least a few minutes of independence. Between the anti nausea drugs and chemotherapy, I felt like I had gotten drunk and then had the crap kicked out of me by ten people. Needless to say the ride home was rough. Too weak to sit up, I laid in the back seat of the car. The anti nausea drugs had begun to wear off. It was impossible to keep my head from swimming and my stomach from turning during the four-hour drive home. I'm sure the drive was more like five or six hours because I kept asking my dad to pull over so I could regain my bearings to prevent myself from throwing up. When we finally got home the only thing I wanted to do was go to sleep in my own bed. With all the aches and pains I was feeling it was like I had the worst case of the flu in the world. Trying to get comfortable enough to get some sleep was difficult.

Hair Today Gone Tomorrow

A few days later I went to the office of Dr. G. who would be overseeing the rest of my treatment. The thing I remember most about our meeting is when I asked him what the chances were that my hair would fall out—a side effect I heard was common with chemotherapy. He said about 90%. The loss of my hair would be a dramatic change in any case, but my hair was short on top like a flat top and reached the middle of my shoulder blades in back. Baldness would obviously be the polar opposite of that.

When we got back from the doctor, I said, "Mom I've got an idea. Before my hair falls out I want to go to a T-shirt shop and get a hat and shirt made that says, "CHEMO SUCKS!" My brother, Chris, chuckled at this notion, and my mom thought it was a neat idea, so off we went. I explained to the gentleman who was helping us why I wanted this, and he was more than happy to assist us. I got a matching shirt and baseball cap both dark blue in color with bold white letters ironed on them. I told my mom I would wear them like badges of honor.

That night my siblings went out with their friends, and my parents wanted to go out to dinner. But I wasn't up to it. My mom was reluctant to go because she wasn't comfortable leaving me alone. I assured her I would be fine. She gave me the name of the restaurant where they would be and gave me a hug and kiss telling me they wouldn't be gone long.

I was sitting there watching television and remembered what the doctor had said about the probability of my hair falling out. Out of curiosity I ran my hand down the back of my head and grabbed a hand-ful of the longest portion of my hair. I gently pulled but didn't feel any pulling on my scalp so I thought my hand was just running down the length of my hair. When I looked at my hand, my eyes sprung open "Oh my God!" I said in shock.

I had a handful of hair that looked like I'd just cut a horse's tail off. I quickly walked to the bathroom and threw that handful in the garbage. I then sat on the edge of the toilet and kept pulling. I couldn't believe how easily it was all coming out. It was like it was all just sitting on my head completely unattached from my scalp. It was so loose that I didn't know how much had come out until I looked at how much I was hold-ing. This is outrageous, I kept thinking to myself. I kept pulling for the next hour or so until no more would come out. By the time I had fin-ished, all that was left was two or three very thin tufts of hair on the front and back of my head. I was at least 95% bald. I hadn't looked in the mirror yet, but I could tell just by feeling my head how much was gone. I was about to look when I heard my parents come through the front door. My mom called out and asked where I was. I heard her walk-ing down the hall towards the bathroom. "Stop right there," I shouted before she could reach the door. "I want you to prepare yourself." "Are you bald?" she asked. She's always had tremendous instincts. "Yes, very." I replied. She slowly peaked around the corner and said "Oh, that's not too bad." I stood up and looked in the mirror. "Oh my God!" I said again as my eyes sprung open with surprise. I looked like Charlie Brown. I was so amazed at how in just one hour it all fell out. No one had prepared me for that. I thought it was going to take weeks.

It was pretty late by then, and I'd had quite enough for one day, so I went to bed. My mom decided to check on me before she turned in for the night. She poked her head around the door and asked if I was okay. I told her I was fine.

It was hard to fall asleep at first because my head didn't feel quite right. The pillowcase was cold against my bare head. It wasn't until I had the idea of lying a towel over my pillow that I was finally able to fall asleep.

The next morning I woke up around nine o'clock and called my girlfriend "J". I told her about my dramatic change in appearance, to which she asked, "It'll grow back right?" "Of course." I replied. She didn't seem too concerned after that.

I asked her if she wanted to go out and do something together. We decided to see a movie, and we invited my mother to come with us. My mom graciously agreed to serve as our banker for that afternoon. The movie wasn't until later that day, but I went to pick up "J" early so we could spend some time together beforehand. When I arrived, her mother greeted me at the door and asked me how I was doing. "Fine," I said. "Nice hat," she remarked with a smirk on her face.

I went inside for a few minutes while "J" finished getting ready. While her mother and I sat on the couch talking, her six-year-old sister walked into the room and sat down next to me. She looked at my head curiously and started reaching for my hat. I gently took her hand before she could take it off. As I did that she quietly asked, "Is your hair gone?" "Yes it is" I said. She asked where it had gone because she had seen me a week earlier with a full head of long hair.

I didn't know how to explain cancer and chemotherapy to her, so I searched quickly for an answer I thought she would understand. I asked her if she had squirrels in her yard. She replied that she did. I went on to explain that behind my house there is a big field with a lot of squirrels in it. Many of the squirrels used up all the grass and sticks to make their nests in the trees and left two of the squirrels without anything to make their nests with. So I went to them and told them they could use my hair because I had a lot of it, and it would grow back. "Really?" she asked with interest and a little bit of doubt.

I think she half believed me. At that same time, my sweetheart had finished getting ready, so we left and headed back to my house to hang out until it was time to leave for the movie.

When we arrived, my mom greeted us and called to my sister, Melissa, who was still in her room. My mom told her to come see my new look. Melissa hadn't seen me since the day before when I still had hair, as I had gone to bed before she got home.

When she came out, I was sitting on the couch next to my girlfriend with my bald head covered by my CHEMO SUCKS! hat. All I said was "Hi sis." She took one look at me and covered her mouth with her hands as she said, "Oh my God."

She burst into tears and ran back to her room. My mother and I looked at each other with surprise. "What happened?" I asked in shock. My mom went to Melissa's room to see if she was all right. I was startled by her reaction and even felt a little guilty for upsetting her. About a half-hour later Melissa came out of her room and gave me a hug. She said "I'm not upset. I was shocked. I didn't expect to see that."

I told her I understood. A few hours later we left for the movies. Things went okay for the next couple of weeks. I spent most of my time at home and with my girlfriend "J". The people around me, my family mostly, seemed to be adjusting pretty well to the changes that were taking place. I hadn't spoken to anyone else about the fact that my cancer had returned because everything had happened too fast and I was more interested in staying close to home where I felt the most safe. It was now time to go to our local hospital to begin my next round of chemotherapy. During this next week my life began a rapid decline.

Round Two

The first round of chemotherapy had claimed the hair on my head, and I was also experiencing a progressive decline in my strength. Over the two weeks since I had left Indiana, I'd been able to regain a good amount of stability in my life again. As my mother drove me to the hospital, the memories of my previous hospital stay quickly resurfaced, and

I became very anxious. I was frightened of being repeatedly violated again and quickly began to develop an attitude of defiance.

After arriving at the hospital and being admitted for treatment, my mom and I were directed to the room where I'd be staying. Ironically as the elevator doors opened onto the floor I was to exit, there was Dr. G. waiting to get on. He paused and took one look at my CHEMO SUCKS! hat and shirt and busted out laughing. He then looked at my face and realized who I was. I did look considerably different from when he last saw me. He grabbed a fellow physician, who was standing nearby, and said, "You gotta see this kid."

They both had a good chuckle from the manner in which I chose to express my feelings. They both remarked how my statement really hit the nail on the head. My doctor asked if he could borrow my hat for a few minutes to go show it to some other doctors. I didn't mind showing it off, so I let him take it. My mother retrieved it a little while later.

As I was getting comfortable (as much as possible) in my hospital bed, an attractive young lady walked in and introduced herself as Laura. She said she would be my nurse during the day for that week. I was a little testy that day, so when she asked if she could get me anything, my response was, "You can undo your shirt one more button."

My mom laughed, as she understood I was joking, but Laura's jaw dropped and her face turned beet red. I told her I was just joking, and my mother spoke to her later so she would take no offense. It turns out that no offense was taken. It was the bluntness of the remark that caught her off guard. I'm ashamed of what I said to her that day. It wasn't the best way to start things off with her. I guess this was just a juvenile attempt on my part to take charge of the situation. When she walked into the room I remembered how I felt the first time I was there after my testicle was removed and how insecure and embarrassed I felt every time a nurse entered the room. I suppose I got a little defensive. I quickly realized how much I would have to depend on her and changed my tune after that.

I tried to stay positive, but this was the week reality really began to hit me—and it hit really hard. I was being given chemotherapy daily, and with each passing hour, I began to feel worse. Again, the anti nausea drugs put me in a stupor that left me unable to comprehend much of what was going on around me. I would wake up each morning (if I'd slept) and find my sheets covered with hair. I was beginning to lose all of my body hair—and I do mean all. My eyebrows and eyelashes thinned, and whenever I blew my nose the nose hairs blew out as well. My sheets had to be changed a few times a day because I was shedding worse than a cat. I wasn't prepared for all of this, and I was quickly becoming extremely self-conscious, more ashamed, embarrassed and very angry. Everything was changing faster than I knew how to deal with.

It was impossible to sleep because my room was only a door down from the nurse's station, which was never quiet. Every hour or so someone would come in to check my IV and always moved my arm to do it. Then at five in the morning, every morning, someone came in and abruptly turned the light on to take my blood. This barrage of inconsideration dealt by the hospital was wearing down my resolve. Between lack of sleep, the head-to-toe nausea and the constant poking and prodding, I began to feel like this whole process was my enemy.

I had been put into a hospital that was supposed to help me get better. Instead I was dressed in a gown that barely covered me and was embarrassing to wear as I was forced to moon the world with every turn. I was denied sleep and all privacy. Nearly everyone who came through my door was a stranger who was there to administer pain or probe my body in a humiliating way. I felt like I had no say in my life anymore as I was repeatedly told by my nurses and doctors that I had to endure this treatment to get better.

The icing on the cake occurred during my fourth day there. I discovered that my regular nurse Laura was off when a nurse I didn't recognize came into my room and hung the bags of chemotherapy along with a few other medications on my IV pole. A few minutes later I began shaking uncontrollably and felt like I was freezing. I felt like the inside of my body was slowly turning to ice. I could literally feel cold flowing through my heart as I curled into a ball to try and stay warm. I began shaking so hard that I pulled several muscles in my legs and back. The pain from this only got worse because I couldn't stop shaking. My mother walked in and saw what was happening. "What's wrong?" she asked in a worried voice. "I'm fffffffreezing" I told her. She brought the nurse in, and they began piling blankets on top of me, which did nothing to stop the freezing or the shaking. Noticing that I was currently receiving intravenous medication my mom asked the nurse what I was being given. The nurse replied that I was given what Dr. G. ordered.

Before we left Indiana, the nurse gave my mother a stack of papers for both her and Dr. G. In that paperwork, which my mother always brought with her to the hospital, was a list of medications I was not to be given because of the negative side effects they would have with my chemotherapy drugs. My mother checked the labels on the bags which where being infused at that time. Sure enough, I was currently being administered a drug that was on that list. My mother quickly ran to the nurse and showed her the list explaining to her what it all meant and frantically asked her to stop the drug. The nurse stated that she didn't have the authority to do that. My mom asked her to call the doctor and tell him what was happening. "Well, we can't question the doctor" was the reply.

My mother repeated that the treatment I was being given was under the direction of the doctors in Indiana and that this new doctor wasn't familiar with it. When the nurse turned a deaf ear, my mother commandeered the use of a hospital phone and called Indiana. She was able to reach the nurse who gave us the paperwork, and when my mother told her what was going on, the nurse shouted, "WHAT?" and asked to talk to my nurse.

After tearing the nurse a new one for not listening to my mother or trying to contact the doctor, she ordered her to, "Pull the medication now."

My mother was able to get back on the phone and talk to the nurse in Indiana one last time while the unconcerned nurse removed the medication. She told my mom that she would personally call my new doctor so that this doesn't happen again. My mother and the new nurse proceeded to take the thick blankets off of me as they were clearly useless since the chills where chemically induced and had nothing to do with temperature. The chills quickly subsided, and I was left in great pain and completely exhausted. The episode had lasted about an hour before the medication was finally stopped. I was left trying to catch my breath and feeling like I'd been run over by every car of a mile—long freight train. I was furious as I saw myself become a victim of my circumstances and what appeared to be an indifferent medical staff. My mother tried to arrange for a hospital social worker to come and see me but was told the hospital was undergoing a reorganization period and one wasn't available. So I was left with no one to talk to to help me deal with my anger and fears. As far as I know, my new doctor never commented on this incident. This demonstrated aloofness on his part, which I would eventually discover was indicative of his bedside manner.

I finished that round of chemo the next day and left for home, still exhausted from what had happened. As soon as I got out of the car and started walking toward the house, a giant wave of nausea hit me, and I stumbled to the bushes in front of the house and proceed to puke my guts out. I felt my mother gently place her hand on my back as she asked if I was all right. "I just have to lie down." I said.

I Reach out for Support

A few days later I began making phone calls to my school friends to finally tell them what was happening and to reach out to them for support. I had made many friends through a youth group before I'd graduated and thought if I could count on anyone, it would be them. We were always saying how we would always be there for each other. I quickly got the impression that the "always" had conditions. After I told them what was happening, they expressed concern, and a few even came to see me over the next week, saying they'd pray for me. Then they disappeared.

When I would phone any of them, I would always get the same responses ...

"I'm too busy to talk now" "I'm just on my way out" or "I have someone over now can I call you back?" They never did. I couldn't understand why they behaved this way. The prayer was nice, but what I really needed was them. Aside from my family, who was already strained by all of this, these were the only people I had to turn to. No one could offer me an explanation for why my loyalty as a friend was being rewarded in this way. I began to feel abandoned and alone. My anger began to turn to rage as I focused on the sense of betrayal I felt. Those around me quickly began to see this. I was becoming more frightened and defensive and in my mind began looking around for whoever was going to hurt me next.

After that week of chemo was over, I brought my anger home, and no one in my house was safe from it. The simple question of how was I feeling was no longer a matter of concern but a condescending remark in my mind, one which guaranteed the asker a "How do you think I feel?" tongue lashing.

I was so hurt by the desertion of the friends I'd cared so much about that I was afraid any sign of concern might be ingenuine and conditional. My family was becoming more and more unsupportive. Unfortunately, I was not raised in a home where problems were met head on. The ostrich mentality, stick your head in the sand and wait for the problem to go away, or say something so mean that the other person gets too angry to continue the conversation, were the prevailing strategies. They were clearly at a loss for how to deal with my illness. My dad found escape in his work, and my siblings were always out with their friends. I understand that this was probably good for them because it helped them maintain normalcy in their own lives. My mom tried her best to be there for me, but she had a whole family to take care of and a business to run, so even she had her limits. Everyone had their limits, and my dear girlfriend "J" was about to reach hers.

The Downward Spiral

I had been throwing my anger around incessantly, and "J" had been able to remain loyal and patient throughout it. She would walk to the hospital every day, which was a short distance from her house, and sit with me for hours. Sometimes she would even fall asleep in the chair. Unfortunately, her family wasn't much different from mine when it came to problem solving, so she was left without anyone to talk to at home. While I valued her support, I was overpowered by the fear that I would lose it, as I had lost everyone else's. The anger brought about by this fear is what I believe to be the main cause of what happened next. I would call her at home, but she wouldn't stay on the phone long. I sensed she was purposely distancing herself from me. After about a week of this, I confronted her with my belief that she was avoiding me, and she laid into me with horribly, cutting words. The one statement in her barrage of anger that stands out the most in my mind is when she said "I never loved you, I was infatuated. Now get over it and get on with your life."

I was devastated. I tried mailing her some letters, but there was no response. At the time all I could see was the increased anger and betrayal I was feeling. In my mind I had truly lost everything. The support of my friends, the love of a wonderful girl and a promising future had been ripped away. It appeared that all of the guarantees I'd been given in the relationships in my life were lies, conditional truths and rules that could be changed at the whim of the participants. I was enraged at myself for having been so blind and so vulnerable. I felt physically hideous and foolish for having trusted others. This rage gradually turned into depression and despair as I dwelled on what I saw as a hopeless situation. I concluded that the world was a horrible place that had turned its back on me.

As I sat in the hospital, those feelings kept building until I thought I would burst. I wouldn't discuss them openly because I felt I couldn't trust anyone. But I had to get them out somehow. Almost from the time I was able to write I found that writing was a safe way to express my feelings. I could be honest without the risk of criticism. Luckily, there was a pad of paper and a pen in the nightstand drawer next to my hospital bed. I picked them up and began writing. At first all I did was write lines of profanity to try and get my anger out. Then I would crumple up the paper and throw it away, hoping my anger would go with it. But that didn't work. I decided to write about my actual feelings to clear my head a little. I wrote about how miserable I was feeling.

"I am walking through a snowstorm and can't see past a foot in front of me. My spirit feels cold and distraught. The sky is gray and the sunlight seems to be hiding from me. I feel like I am walking a long distance that is all uphill. The snow is so thick I felt like I'm getting nowhere. My heart feels cold, empty and smothered in pain. The cold wind is blowing, and my spirit is growing colder. My fire for life is slowly burning out. I feel like I'm in a pit surrounded by walls of ice impossible to climb. I feel trapped. My only companion is deep depression. I feel that all life has left for me is death."

It didn't seem that there was a life left for me. I was consumed only by the life I'd lost. There were some around me who tried to make an effort to comfort me, but at that point I was no longer willing to listen. I had shrunk into a cocoon of self-pity and doubt. My head began racing with thoughts of

"Why me?"

"What the hell did I do to deserve this?"

"How dare they do this to me?"

"Why do I bother living?"

"Why can't I just die?" I was sliding deeper and deeper into depression. Although I was told that week of chemo would be my last, I found no comfort in it, as I had given up on life. I had realized that all of the lessons and truths that I had clung to were not the absolutes I'd been encouraged to see them as. I'd always thought that if I lead a good life, nothing bad would ever happen to me and that if I were there for others, they'd be there for me. Nothing I had ever learned in church or at school could ever have prepared me for this.

I was becoming suicidal, and this was the most terrifying feeling I'd ever known. I couldn't trust how I saw others, so I lost faith in who I thought I was. I was lost. I sat alone in my hospital bed and at the very moment I needed someone the most, Laura walked in. She simply asked how I was doing and I burst into tears. She sat on the side of my bed and held my hand while I cried.

"What's wrong?" she asked.

"Everything's wrong" I answered. "Everything. Why me? Why did this have to happen to me? I don't know what to do."

She looked at me with compassion in her eyes, but behind her compassion, I could tell she was feeling helpless in that moment. Although all she could say is that things will get better, her being there when I needed someone, if only for a few minutes, was a tremendous gift.

When I was finally able to go home, I locked myself in my room and pulled all the shades. I spent the next week crying and sometimes yelling. My parents were frightened because they didn't know what to do for me. In my mind I kept rehashing all that had happened. I needed to let it out another way because yelling was making me hoarse. I got so enraged at one moment that I cocked my arm and punched a hole in my bedroom wall. When I later looked in the hole I noticed that my hand had barely passed between two boards. Had I been even a little off, I probably would have broken my hand.

I realized that I was clearly out of control and sat down trying to catch my breath and regain some composure. I saw one of my old notebooks across the room and decided to focus my energies again on writing what I was feeling. So I picked up my pen and began writing about the sense of betrayal I was feeling. I began with how this all started with a lump.

"My doctor soon said it was cancer. He thought he got it all, but he didn't. Then the cancer came back. He told me these treatments would make it better, but things got worse. I turned to my friends for support. I had stood by them after all. But they turned their backs on me. They treated me like a ghost—like I was already a name on a tombstone. As the treatment increased, so did my pain and my tears."

I had contemplated suicide several times throughout my ordeal but never once tried it. Something in the back of my mind kept saying don't do it. Just wait one more day. Maybe it will change. Nothing on the surface was changing, but still, something was holding me up. What made me want to give up? What made me want to stay?

At some point I began stubbornly refusing to let what was happening to me ruin my life. I was tired of feeling this way, and no one around me seemed to have any answers. I was not going to allow all of the negativity of the situation beat me. I was tired of not having any control. It was time to start asking myself some serious questions. Again, I wrote it all out.

"Is my life worth living? Does my life have a meaning? Is my being here significant or just a brief flicker in the sky? Is life about all the material things? If so, life can be taken away from me? If life is about the things we all can enjoy, then life won't ever go away. I need life to be about the things that don't wear out, that are timeless and have endurance. Before now I valued the temporary things and was let down hard. At this moment I ask myself, what am I living for? Is being alive itself the greatest gift? Are material things required to make it worth living? Right now it seems life is all I have. I have to start somewhere. I'm still uncertain as to why I should stay. But there is no denying, for some reason, I chose to stay today."

In spite of the fact I'd immersed myself in hopelessness, it became evident that something was going to have to give. I realized that the question "Why me?" could not be answered.

CHAPTER TWO

From Suffering to Living

"Why me?" was irrelevant. The fact of the matter was that it was me. So the real question was *"Where do I go from here?"* Over the next week I spent enough time in solitude with my feelings of depression to realize they were getting me nowhere. I discovered that the cancer of depression was overtaking me and becoming a bigger problem than the physical one. I began getting sick of feeling miserable. I was eighteen years old, and if I was going to live, I wasn't about to spend the rest of my life living under a cloud. I decided that I'd had enough and was going to find a way to do things differently. I clearly needed more than simply a physical cure. How to do this, however, was unclear. I knew I wanted out of this downward spiral, but my fears of further disappointment and my doubts about life in general left me without a place to begin.

The First Step toward Healing

One day I was sitting in my room, and out of boredom and curiosity, I glanced at my bookshelf where a lot of old books had found their way to collect dust. I noticed a particular book with a Chinese author; the book was called *Tao Te Ching*. I read the back cover, which said the passages in this book were written a few thousand years ago. As I looked through its pages, I found that although the text was written for a time long past, its words slapped me in the face with a stinging relevance. I didn't read the book cover to cover at first but leafed through its pages. One passage in particular was the catalyst I needed to move me in a new direction, and it will forever stick in my mind. It said "The journey of a thousand miles begins with a single step." After reading this my mind began to calm, if only for a moment. The enormity of my circumstances had just been simplified. All I needed to do was start where I was, to take a single step to begin my long journey out of these circumstances. It wasn't a matter of solving everything at once but instead just one step at a time. I was still at a loss for what that step was however. As I read more, it was as if this book had been written for me.

The *Tao Te Ching* It stated that the source of all things gives birth to both good and evil without taking sides. It welcomes both entities as complementary forces in life. It then asks the questions, can you let yourself become as a child? Can you love others without imposing your will? Can you deal with things by letting them take their course? Can I have without wanting to possess? Can I act without expectation and without desire to control? For this is the way of peace and virtue. I had found the key to my journey back.

These few passages seemed to answer my most biting questions. It was fortunate that I was looking for these answers when I stumbled across them. Until this point I was caught in a whirlwind of selfishness. I was consumed by beliefs about how others were supposed to give me what I wanted from them and were to meet my expectations. I had been fighting this whole process and trying to keep my life as it had been, failing to allow it to take its own course. I discovered that starting over meant not having back what I had lost – an important lesson considering there was no way I could get back what the cancer had already taken from me. I had to learn to deal with the change that was rapidly present in my life and learn how to use it to my advantage instead of fearing and resenting it. Of course the book made it all sound so simple. But how was I supposed to learn to implement this in my life? I was frightened before when faced with the loss of a belief system that had suddenly become inapplicable to my life. Even more frightening now was the thought of learning to trust a new one.

The Hara Decision

I had to take an important step. I had to put it all on the line and reach down into my gut ("Hara" in Japanese) to find out if this was the right direction for me to go. This step is a powerful first step in curing the fear that compels you to hang onto the security of your old ways of thinking. As I mentioned, the time came when I knew I had to radically change my way of thinking, and it was at that moment that I made what I now call a "Hara decision." Let me first differentiate between other types of decisions. A decision made with your mind is strong but often lacks the rigor to hold up against mental fatigue, frustration, confusion, the influence of others or simple everyday distractions. Many of us take our cues and are guided by forces outside of ourselves, which leaves room for the introduction of doubt into the picture. As such, a person looking for direction outside of oneself is less likely to stick with a decision very long when his or her environment resists his or her efforts.

A heartfelt decision causes you to lead with emotions and is often impulsive, which can leave you open to pain, suffering and eventually defeat. Guided by good intentions, you often stop when your intentions are rebuked and your feelings get hurt.

A "Hara decision" is the most powerful decision you can make. This kind of decision is one that rises from the very core of your being. Most people understand it as our "gut feeling" or instinct. In Japanese medicine as well as in many martial arts systems, the Hara is the area three inches below your navel and as many inches inward. It is the center of your body—your center of gravity as well as the center of your spirit. While you walk down the street, it is your Hara that keeps you physically balanced, upright and steady. The direction your Hara points in is the direction you're walking in. As such it guides you in all matters. It is easier to push someone off balance when they are bent over because their Hara is pointing toward the ground. When pushed, their Hara leads them in the direction it is pointing.

When something feels dangerous and you get an uneasy feeling in your gut, that is your Hara talking. Your spiritual center tells you when something threatens your balance physically, mentally and spiritually. But most important, it tells you when something feels right and is the right thing to do. When you experience this feeling, you can be sure that it has a high level of certainty. It is an intrinsic and ancient compass that life gives us for our own protection and guidance. If you follow the guidance of your Hara and trust that "gut feeling" from the center of who you are, you can be certain your decisions will be correct and lead you toward what is right for you.

When your decisions come from your Hara, they will always stem from who you are. They become a part of you and an expression of your inner wisdom that knows the direction you need to be going. Once you have made a Hara decision to pursue something, accomplishing it becomes as essential as breathing. Your guidance is not derived solely from external cues or by impulse. Instead you are driven by an internal well of commitment and passion that is the source of what defines you. I was so desperate for answers and change that my commitment for something better was as strong as the commitment someone might have in trying to escape a burning house. As such, a Hara decision is so powerful and focused that it has no doubt.

I had made the Hara decision that life as I currently knew it was intolerable, and I was going to make it into what I wanted it to be. I was going to find control again where I could. I was going to be in charge of my life and my future. Hopelessness wasn't acceptable, and I wouldn't stop until I had the best life I could make for myself. I pointed my Hara, my whole being, in the direction of my goal, and, therefore, I would only stop doing what's best for me when my life stops. This decision was the most powerful step in beginning the process of getting out of my own way.

Isolation

Over the next week I studied the *Tao Te Ching* in greater depth and began gaining a little more enthusiasm about a positive future. As my mental resolve strengthened, I felt my physical health begin to slowly deteriorate even more. I was starting to get very sick, unlike anything I'd experienced to this point. A high fever, a burning sore throat and a stomachache quickly developed. My complexion became pale white. My mother had observed this progression as well, but we hoped these were only side effects of the chemotherapy and would soon pass. Quietly I feared my cancer had become more aggressive. Toward the end of the week, I was bed ridden. I was coughing and my throat was so sore that I couldn't eat anything or even swallow my own saliva. Speaking was difficult, and I felt pain in every inch of my body. Finding a comfortable position was absolutely impossible. I felt like I was going to die.

My mother called Dr. G. to tell him what was happening and asked if she should take me to the hospital. He thought there was a chance that my white blood cell count had dropped due to the chemotherapy, which would leave me unable to fight off infection. He discounted this possibility however, because his experience told him that if this were going to happen, it would have happened long before. He was the expert, so my mother sat with me for the next couple of hours, doing her best to keep me comfortable and ride this out. By then I had had enough and told my mom to take me to the hospital. I didn't care what the doctor said; I only knew how I felt. My mom and my sister helped me to the car, and mom drove me to the emergency room.

I waited for over an hour in the waiting room, where I almost fainted twice. My mom repeatedly went to the reception desk and begged to have me seen more quickly but to no avail. While I sat there trying to muster up some strength, I had an experience that brought a huge smile to my face and also shed some light on things. Sitting in the chairs across from me was a Mexican man and his son who couldn't have been older than three years old. They where waiting for the boy's mother, who I discovered later had come in to have an injury to her arm looked at. The little boy was fascinated by my appearance. Here I sat as pale as glue with practically no body hair to speak of. The boy stared at me awestruck like he was seeing a ghost, which wasn't too far off. He looked me right in the face and pointed at me with one hand as he touched his own head with the other, saying to his father with amazement,

"No pelo No pelo."

Which meant "No hair No hair."

His father tried to quiet him, but I could only smile and gesture to his father that it was quite all right. My mother had overheard this and understood enough Spanish to know what the boy was saying and to explain to his father why I looked this way. The father gave me a smile of encouragement as he talked with his boy. By the time the boy's mother returned, it was finally my turn to be seen.

I was taken back and laid on a cart where the E.R. doctor came over to me and introduced herself. My mother gave her my medical history, which was written all over me by then. In spite of what my doctor had said, she told us she would order a blood test in order to get my white cell count. About half an hour later the doctor came back with the results and said that I would be staying. She explained that I had a condition called neutropenia, which is doctor talk for a low white blood cell count.

My white count had not only dropped; it had dropped a lot. Where the normal count was about 4,000, mine had dropped to 700. With so little immunity to fight with, I had contracted a systemic infection that caused both my esophagus and my stomach to become inflamed. I hadn't eaten in several days because swallowing had been too painful, so to remedy the pain the doctor mixed up a cocktail of antacid and an anesthetic called xylocaine for me to drink. It was like trying to swallow toothpaste, and its affects wore off about 15 minutes after I swallowed it. Then I had to wait another hour for an isolation room to be sterilized before I was admitted to the hospital.

It was about one in the morning when I was finally taken to my room. My mother left with plans to return first thing in the morning. A nurse got me settled in bed and then left the room. Physically I was the worst I had ever been. I felt like I had been dropped from an airplane without a parachute. A few minutes later my stomach had decided that it didn't like the doctor's little cocktail. I quickly grabbed a basin, which was luckily within reach on my nightstand, and proceeded to vomit for the next ten minutes. I barely had time to inhale before I would vomit again. It hurt so badly that it felt like I was throwing up razor blades. My throat might as well have been torn out of my body. It took me a while to catch my breath, after which I collapsed asleep from exhaustion. It seems that a lot of my rest during these months was gained only at the hands of exhaustion.

The next morning around five or six I was rudely awaken. I felt someone nudging my shoulder, and heard a male voice saying,

"Hey, wake up."

It was Dr. G. "the expert" whose bedside manner left a lot to be desired. His attitude was pretty cancerous at that moment. All I could do was look at him and wish I had the strength to punch him out. This was the second time his expertise had made my suffering worse. The first time by having a drug administered to me that he had been instructed not to give me under any circumstances. He looked at my test results and said,

"It looks like your white cells took a nosedive."

He didn't apologize for making a mistake; he didn't admit he was wrong for telling my mother that there was no way that this was the problem. Perhaps his ego couldn't handle the idea that he was human. I would have respected him greatly had he admitted his error; instead, I resented him. All he did was tell me that I would be staying there while intravenous antibiotics were pumped into me to fight off the infection. This would give my white blood cells a chance to replenish themselves. Until my count was high enough to provide me with sufficient immunity, I would have to stay isolated.

I had been placed in reverse isolation, which meant I was in a sterile room by myself where I would be protected from everyone else who might have germs. Everyone had to scrub their arms up to the elbow and wear a mask a gown and surgical gloves if they wanted to enter my room. This was difficult to endure. I was denied human contact except through sterile rubber gloves and masks and that contact was usually from nurses or someone who woke me up to poke me with a needle. My mother couldn't even give me a hug.

Every morning at five someone came into my room to draw blood so they could check my white cell count and see how I was doing. At this point I had only one good vein left in my right arm to draw blood from. Throughout my various hospital stays, my IVs had been started and restarted so many times that by the end of my chemotherapy experience, every major vein in both of my forearms and hands were scorching hot with inflammation, a condition called phlebitis. The veins on the top, bottom and sides of both arms were so swollen that they stuck out like the veins on a bodybuilder's arm. But mine were red, swollen and too painful to even touch. The one remaining vein that was being used to draw blood from had been poked so many times that you could actually see a circle of holes that weren't being given a chance to heal. Between my phlebitis and puncture holes, I looked like a heroin junkie.

I felt and looked like garbage and was in so much pain that even the weight of my blankets was sometimes too much to bear. The antibiotics slowly seemed to start working, and my white count slowly climbed back to a healthy level. Although this physical isolation made me feel even more emotionally isolated, being alone was the very catalyst I needed to take that first step on my thousand-mile journey.

The Lesson of the Clock

As I had committed myself to finding control where I could, my mind was focused on any opportunity to learn something new that I could use to speed me on my way. Like I said, a Hara decision is like a commitment to breathing—it's difficult to take your mind off of it. I was more focused and alert, as my mind was so eager. Just as a hungry person is more adept at smelling the slightest hint of cooking food.

Toward the middle of the week, the isolation was really getting to me. It was so quiet that I could hear the ticking of the clock that hung on the wall directly across from me. Its face appeared to be staring me down. I began to study it, tick-tock, tick-tock. I then looked out my window and saw cars driving by. I heard a train roll by and saw airplanes overhead. Time was moving on, going forward, tick-tock, tick-tock. Time wouldn't stop. The world was going on without me. If I were to die the world would be just fine. The world wouldn't stop just because I did. The hands of the clock would continue to turn, and the world would keep on turning. This was an incredibly humbling realization.

When the only activity available to me was to watch time pass, it was easy to see it happening without me. Amazing how an everyday object like a clock can be such a valuable learning tool. From then on I began looking at everyday experiences differently. I figured if a clock could teach me so much, what else was out there waiting for me? After the lesson of the clock, I could no longer maintain a sense of self-importance. I could no longer justify the idea that my expectations ought to have been met by those I felt betrayed me. I now knew that I wasn't so important that I couldn't be done without. I realized that my friends quite possibly chose to do without me instead of dealing with my circumstances and me. I was still upset about it, but it was beginning to make sense. I could no longer sit and hold them responsible for supplying the emotional support I needed. This psychological tumor was beginning to shrink.

A few weeks earlier I had come to the conclusion that something was going to have to give. I just realized that that something was me—I was going to have to give to myself. I was going to have to be responsible. I was going to have to find, within myself, the support I needed to get through this. I would make a commitment to treat myself well, always and in every way.

Along with an increase in white blood cells, my various blood tests also revealed that my cancer was gone. I was in remission, which meant there was no sign of cancer anywhere in my body. With the news that I was going to live finally confirmed, I realized more than ever that I would have to get with the program and learn how to live all over again.

For once in a long time I began to feel in charge again. No longer was there anyone or anything to blame for how I was feeling. I decided I would take responsibility for that. Where everything else in my life had fallen short, I was going to have to rise to the occasion to make sure everything would turn out the best it could. A lot had happened that I couldn't change, but no longer was I viewing these things as obstacles. I would instead use them as building blocks. I figured, so what if life had thrown me a pile of horse crap? I was going to do what was necessary to turn the poop into fertilizer and grow a beautiful garden.

With this new resolve of spirit and will, I had made an additional Hara decision that would shape the rest of my life. From now on the story of my life would change from victim to victor. Victimization was the role I'd played since this whole thing began and you see where that got me. I was no longer going to allow others to decide how I feel about myself or allow circumstances to be bigger than me. I would no longer let life happen to me. I was going to start happening to it. In the best way I knew how.

My life was starting over now, and in the new story I needed to be the hero, the victor. I know now that my old life hadn't ended, because there are no endings, only transitions and new beginnings. But my decision did help release the confidence I needed to go after what I wanted in life.

As I lay in my hospital bed, basking in my new resolve, I closed my eyes and tried to rest a little. I began taking some slow, deep breaths. I did so in an attempt to relax and alleviate some of the physical pain I was feeling and hopefully to take my mind off of it for a while. The room was very silent, and all I could hear was the clock. As I started to relax more, my breathing became less deliberate and took over for itself. I just laid there and paid attention to my breathing as my chest rose and fell. I began relaxing deeper and deeper and felt the preoccupation with my pain diminish as I found comfort in the depth of my breath. I found to some degree that I was actually able to relax my pain away.

As I felt my breathing change, I remembered what the *Tao Te Ching* had said about how life was in a state of perpetual change. I could hear the clock ticking as I felt the rising and falling of my chest. This constant changing of my breath was the changing of life; it was this change that was sustaining my life. As time changed and passed, so did my breath and so did my life. I began seeing that as I had been resisting change, I was actually resisting life, because change was the force that was sustaining my life at this very moment. As my chest rose and fell, as my heart beat in my chest, so did the rhythm of life.

I began thinking about all of the things I had lost in the past that had caused me so much pain and about all of the things in the future that I feared I would never have. I never thought for a moment that everything I needed depended on what was happening right now, this moment. I was alive because of the present changing of my breath and the beating of my heart. I didn't need to worry about the past, because it had changed and become the present. The future isn't even here yet, so what in the world can I do about that? I had enough to worry about in the present. My own breath had shown me where I was at in life and who I was. I am here, I am now, and this is where I must begin my journey. I opened my eyes and sat up. I started contemplating all of those everyday things I hadn't given proper attention to because of my preoccupations with the befores and afters of my life. I then reached over to the nightstand, grabbed my pad of paper and began writing. The tumors of clinging to the past and longing for the future were beginning to shrink.

"I look around this very moment. What do I see? I see the brightness of the sunshine, clouds passing overhead, my reflection in the window. What do I hear? I hear the joyful singing of a bird, a plane flying overhead, people talking and laughing outside my room. The wind rustling through the trees, the sound of my own heartbeat, the calm of my own breath."

"Where am I right now, this very moment? Where is all of this taking place? I am in the present. This is where my life is taking place, where it's unfolding. Nowhere else." "The seeds of my past have blossomed into where I am now. But I cannot climb back into a seed; I must either continue to grow or give up and die. I must give in or win. Complacency is the enemy of growth. So growth is my choice."

"I have been hanging on to the anger and sadness of the past. Hindering my own growth in the present. Longing for the pleasures of the past as well as clinging to its sorrows. Never once trying to do anything now."

"From this moment on I will make a commitment to myself. Once the present moment passes, it becomes the past, so I will let it go. This is an essential rule of life that I've missed until now. Now I will embody it as one of my greatest assets, so I will not be distracted from the life in front of me. I promise to let the moment pass, and any anger, fear and sadness that came with it. These feelings may have been relevant in that moment, but the moment is gone. Why keep these feelings now? I will never again stand in the way of my own experience of the full joy and happiness of life. For how can I enjoy life, if I am never here?"

This was an incredible revelation that was amazingly therapeutic to write. If I was going to achieve my goal of a better life, I had to be constantly aware of what the current situation provided for me. I had to keep my eye out for the clock and any other resource I could tap into on my journey. I believe that if my life hadn't unfolded in this way, I may not have achieved this realization. Having lost confidence in my past and approaching a doubtful future, the present was all I had left. I learned that I can always count on the present, because it will always be here with plenty of opportunities. I now realized that where I was today was the best and most important place to be. I felt a little anxious at the prospects before me. Although I had wanted to be free of this depression for so long, it seemed to be leaving a little more quickly than I thought it would. This was a little unnerving, as it seemed too good to be true. I returned my attention to the comfort of my breath, which had calmed me so well before, and just enjoyed the experience.

The Bending of the Tree

As I began to feel more at ease, I turned and looked out my window. I looked beyond the road and into the forest preserve, which was carpeted with trees. I was very mindful of the present moment as I watched the branches swaying in the gentle breeze. Inspired by the clock, I was on the lookout for whatever my surroundings could teach me. I suddenly recalled what I had read about not trying to control change but allowing it to take its course. So I closely observed how the trees kept adjusting to the breeze, back and forth, back and forth. I was struck by the spontaneity and resilience of the branches as they gently swayed. I realized that the trees were living in the present moment as they embraced and adjusted to the changing breeze.

In these few moments I learned how I needed to deal with the adversity that I was faced with. For so long my coping skills were tainted by overreaction, anticipation and clinging to the past—the very skills the tree eloquently did without. Instead, it bent only as much as necessary; it didn't resist the oncoming breeze and didn't stay bent in anticipation that the wind might blow again. The tree dealt only with what needed to be dealt with as it arose. As I watched the tree, to me it became even clearer how being concerned with past losses and future gains was irrelevant in dealing with the present. Although the past often plays a role in most people's lives, it is how we adjust to it in the present that is the key.

For the next few days I sat on this discovery and let it take root. I kept watching the trees and relaxing with my breath. I now realized more than ever that the solutions I needed were all around me. Right outside my window in fact. The problems I was having were life problems more than they were human problems. Other living things were and are dealing with the same struggles as I was; I need only look to them for solutions.

After seven days in isolation, I was able to convince the doctor to let me go home. My white cell count was only a little over 1,000, but the doctor was willing to let me go because I was feeling better and agreed to take special precautions to help prevent against getting sick again. I left the hospital with the first smile that anyone had seen on my face in months.

Over the next couple of days at home, I stayed inside and read what I had written over the past week. I was amazed how through a simple process in nature, I was beginning to unlearn the expectations I had developed based on past adversity that left me unable to deal with present struggles. I also realized that I was expecting and thus fearing that the pains of the past will continue to occur in the present and the future. It was becoming obvious that I needed to begin looking at my expectations more closely, as they were responsible for so much of the suffering I was now faced with. I needed to see if I could unlearn what I had built in my mind over so many years.

Although thinking this through helped me realize what I had been doing to myself, it would not be an easy task to incorporate all of this into my thinking. My emotions were still pretty raw, and I was still reactionary in many ways in dealing with things. But I had made my decision, and there was no turning back. Having all of this free time to indulge in a deep introspection obviously helped to reinforce the path I was now on. I was feeling much better now physically, and emotionally and mentally I was well on my way. It was amazing how a little hope fueled by an unbreakable commitment can speed your recovery.

I was slowly regaining my strength as my infection disappeared, but I was facing a new experience that sapped my strength. I had held so much anger inside for so many months that I was wiped out after discovering that it was safe to let it go. It takes a lot of strength to hold so much negative energy in, so naturally I was tired after hanging on to it for so long. It seemed that carrying emotional burdens was more tiring than toting physical ones. With no one to blame any longer, there was nothing left to fuel such negativity. It just sort of burnt out like a fire that had been robbed of oxygen.

Beyond feeling stronger, I wasn't so afraid of infection anymore. I looked out the living room window and saw a gorgeous day waiting outside. The sky was clear blue, and as I stuck my head out the door, I felt the nice warm air against my face. I couldn't stay in on a day like this, so I grabbed my pad of paper and walked outside to my backyard. I sat a lawn chair in the middle of the yard and took a seat. I just sat there taking everything in to see what I could discover. Did I ever discover.

So much of what I had thought about life was determined by the conclusions I'd drawn from what I had seen and heard and felt. I believed the obvious to be the truth. Now I looked around more closely at all of nature's colors. I listened. The wind and the trees were rustling. The birds chirping. The grass had never smelled so sweet. I decided to look within my senses to explore what they were telling me and to see if I was hearing, seeing and sensing all that I could. If I weren't, then how could I go about removing the blinders that had led to my misperceptions in the first place?

Previously I had lost the willingness to trust when my friends left me and I found out life wasn't the way I thought it should be. I was learning to trust again as I was finding more about how life could be different. I was finding life to be more tolerant and forgiving than I had been. More flexible and resilient than I had learned to be. I was learning—learning to be more alive. I opened my senses and my mind and began to see what I could experience. As I experienced, I also wrote.

"I used to only look with my eyes, which made it difficult to see. Perhaps if I look a little longer, a little deeper, I might find the truth underneath. It is so easy to become distracted by the colors or the shapes and forget to look beyond them. It's important to note the labels I use and the values I place. How much of my life is not a result of how things are, but more what I do with how things are?"

"It's beginning to look like things are at their best before I smear my impressions all over them. From now on it's experience first, interpretation second. When I do them simultaneously, the interpreting often gets ahead of the experience when prejudice kicks in."

"My ears need to listen more closely, more thoroughly. Then maybe I'll truly hear. I'll look beyond the loudness and the noise, listening for what's being said instead of for what I want to hear. Hopefully things will come across more clearly. Once my senses fall in line, or more to the point, my mind's interpretation of what my senses give it. Then my life will continue to improve, as the accuracy of what it's taking in increases."

For so long I had been a victim of the blindness of superficiality. Taking things for how they appeared and failing to look more deeply. It was amazing how much more there was to be experienced when I wasn't hastily assembling things according to my preferences and personal judgements. My experience with cancer taught me that things in life occur in one of two ways: They happen either how I intend them to happen or how they actually happen. My preferences and expectations had nothing to do with whether I got cancer or not. Of course I would have preferred not to have suffered this way. But preferences aside, what actually happened is what I was left to deal with. As I began studying my experiences more, I was becoming more aware of what was actually happening before me. I realized that I needed to stop seeing what I liked and didn't like or how I could make a situation go in my favor. Instead of only looking for what I wanted, I could just pay attention to the things around me, and I would soon discover the things I never even knew I needed. Had I not been paying attention, I may have missed them.

The Lesson of the Leaf

My mind was spinning with all this new information now that I was paying closer attention. Life may be capable of going on without me, but since I would not be leaving anytime soon, I needed to find a way to jump back into the life stream.

As I sat in the yard trying to figure out just where I fit into the scheme of things, my eyes began to wander around the yard. I noticed the leaves on the trees rustling in the breeze; my attention was soon drawn to a single leaf hanging from a branch overhead. I watched it as it danced around, with the sunlight flickering through. It was at that moment that it hit me. I remembered what I had learned in school about the role the sun plays in photosynthesis, which is a process plants go through to produce the oxygen in the air I was breathing at that moment. During photosynthesis, in addition to the sunlight, the tree utilizes the carbon dioxide exhaled by living, breathing things like myself. I just realized how important I was in the scheme of things, in the process of life.

The more I thought about it the more I realized how as I sat there, I was an active part of this symphony of interdependence being played in this very moment. The leaf and I couldn't survive without each other, and neither of us could exist without the sun. When I looked at a leaf or even myself, I realized that I was looking at a reflection of everything else.

I'd never felt so insignificant and yet so essential in my whole life. I had to give my mind a breather as I was getting a little ahead of myself. I went inside and took a nap, as I was still pretty weak. Even sitting outside in the heat was enough to exhaust me. When I awoke, I got something to eat and started again. I felt a trembling in my gut as I contemplated giving up the old ideas I'd been clinging to for so long. My Hara was in the process of a major change in direction. In spite of my nervousness, the excitement I was feeling from all of these new life-affirming discoveries made any fears pale by comparison. My commitment was bigger than my fears. I began to remember what I had read in the *Tao Te Ching*, and started again to ask myself those very important questions.

A Child's Eyes

Could I let myself become like a child? After having been through so much could I find innocence again? I had to learn to see everything for the first time again. I quickly realized that after having lost so much of my life in the past, I was essentially starting over. I had already begun the process of throwing out my old ideas and starting fresh. I was more or less a beginner.

I remembered the little boy I encountered in the waiting room who was in awe of my baldness. He was a child learning about life. I watched my young niece Jessica playing; she was so full of enthusiasm, seemingly carefree. How could I once again become this way? How could I proceed without presumption? I quietly looked inside myself to discover just what it meant to me to be a child again, a beginner.

"The eyes of a child are those of a beginner, bright and awake. Watching everything within their view with innocence. Every experience is a new one. A child recognizes this. Without the biases, prejudices and presumptions of a mind cluttered by its own thoughts and agendas."

"A child has an unfettered view of the world. Free from the spots of misperception. Presumption packages reality into its own convenient definition. Bias cuts reality into little pieces, keeping only the ones it wants. Prejudice blinds the eyes, like the moon during an eclipse blinds the brilliant illumination of the sun's eye upon the world."

"A child's eyes are like a mirror. When something is held up to it you see an exact reflection of what it sees. The mirror does not try to change it to suit itself. Neither does the child's eyes; they just accept it. Through a child's eyes all things may pass, all things are equal and all things are special because all things are new. They are life, they are to cherish, and a child does."

"Many minds experience the changing reality before them. Then suddenly, they get in the way of their own experiences. They grab hold of that moment and freeze it within a thought. This thought, often wrapped in presumption, is then clung to and mistaken for reality. Content that this is it, they stop watching."

"No longer keeping a watchful eye on the unfolding reality, but fixating on the frozen, delusive thoughts of their mind. Many thus run to their thoughts for their reality. And true reality rarely gets a chance."

"A child awakens each morning, bright eyed and eager at the unlimited possibilities before it. It knows no limitations. The eyes of the child know only love, compassion and acceptance. Grateful for the experiences of which they are a part, without judgment. How can something new be judged? Why judge? Keep it new. If something is new, then it has no equal, no basis for comparison. Don't freeze it with thought. When life is frozen it dies. Leave it alone, keep it alive. Just watch it; experience it, live it, with a child. As a child."

"The illuminated eyes of a child, that light up all experience, don't question that which is before them, they watch. Its eyes don't doubt, they trust. Its eyes don't fear, they have courage and take risks. The eyes of a child are as full of beauty and wonder as the life in which they actively participate. The eyes of a child are those of a beginner. As the sunrise begins a new day, as each turning of the clock begins twenty-four crisp new hours of life. As each rising and falling of our own breath, provides us with the beginning of one more moment of life."

"Life is always a beginner, new every moment. Each new moment has its tasks to be tended to. The beginner's mind, the beginner's eye of a child. Is only following life's lead. Watch the children. Watch their eyes, watch life unfold through a beginners eyes."

I think now I've got a good idea what it means to be a beginner. Sure children may learn to discriminate eventually. But as an adult I am fully aware that I do it, as well as the trouble it causes. So from now on I am making the decision not to do it. If I do it I will take the time to undo it. Like the leaf I am interdependent with all of the things from which I am made. As I am a product of this vast universe, so is everything else, and everyone else.

I Shall Be the Sun

I can no more be prejudice of another person than I can be of myself. We are simply waves flowing side by side all part of the same ocean with the appearance of being separate. We all smile and cry; we all live and die. We are all warmed and nurtured by the same sun. The sun doesn't discriminate. The sun is part of me, part of you, so why should I discriminate? With pen in hand I contemplated the nondiscriminatory nature of the sun, to see what it could teach me. "As the eyelid on the horizon slowly opens for the dawn, its iris illuminates a new day. The darkness slowly withdraws and life continues on. The rays of the sun envelop all things, rejecting none. It shines upon the pleasure as well as the suffering of this life. I am grateful to the sun for the life it helps create. It does so without judgement. It only patiently provides the support required for all things to grow, adapt and refine themselves. It doesn't hold a standard for who or what is worthy of its warmth. It simply provides an environment in which things can simply be as they are. The sun is not eclipsed by fear; it allows itself and others to shine. The eye of sunshine is crystal clear; perhaps my eyes can be so as well. As the sun sustains my life, I might as well absorb its character as well as its warmth."

Whenever the sun is shining I am reminded to see things as they are—indivisible, equally valuable and in a position to become their best. Being constantly attuned to my minds' attempt at discrimination. I understand that I am not responsible for the fact that I have this life. I owe my existence to those factors that are responsible for it. The sun being one of them. If the sun and other forces have the power to give and sustain life, they must know something about how to live that life. The tree that helps produce oxygen knows a lot about dealing with adversity, and the sun about nondiscrimination. All of life has a lot to teach, and I have a lot to learn.

Time slowly passed, and weeks turned to months as I slowly regained my strength. I continued to sit in the yard and began taking short walks to see what else I could discover about the world through my new eyes.

The Bird of Change

As I got stronger I was able to take longer walks before becoming tired. On several occasions I made my way to the city park. Autumn was coming into being, and I was able to experience the glorious array of colors that defined the season. I was so amazed by the complexity and variety of all the things that, in the past, I may have only regarded in passing. I saw colors I never knew existed because I had no use for them. Sounds that I once avoided, I now appreciated as I allowed them to be instead of preferring them not to be.

I learned a lot in that park over the next month. When I was up to it, I would go and spend hours there. I would look, listen and feel the life around me. I would sit and listen to the animals and feel the wind blow as I felt my breath change from inhalation to exhalation. I closed my eyes as I heard the birds around me engage in a vocal dance. The changing flexion of their vocal cords resulted in a glorious song. It was amazing how this little thing called change could be responsible for so much beauty. I opened my eyes and saw one of the birds fly by. As I watched the grace of its flight, I realized that it was the change in the position of its wings as they met with the air that was responsible for this beauty. Again this wondrous change that I had so often fought against was now becoming my greatest teacher. I was later able to write down my observations.

"All things begin and end with change; thusly, no things begin and end. Change never ends, it is constant. When is time ever frozen? When is there any pause or hesitation during which a thing may begin or end? Change, when embraced, brings peace and harmony because all things inevitably pass. Change, when fought for or against, brings suffering and confusion when we seek to influence that which is out of our control."

"As I watched the bird fly by and thought of my own struggles adapting to change, I pictured a man as he sat in the warm spring grass and observed the beauty and grace of a bird as it flew overhead. He jumped to his feet and ran, hands outstretched, grasping at the bird, trying eagerly to capture it. So that he could obtain the beauty and the grace for himself."

"The man finally collapsed after a long chase. His only rewards were exhaustion and frustration. The man didn't realize that he couldn't capture the change that gave birth to the beauty and the grace. The change ever present in the movement of the bird's wings, as they rise and fall moment to moment."

"This man was unaware of the transient nature of the encounter. The meeting of the path between the man and the bird was temporary. Such is the nature of each moment. The man attempted to cling to the encounter, and in fighting the fleeting and ever-changing moment, he brought suffering into a moment that before contained only grace and beauty."

"The following day, the man again sat in the spring grass, and again the bird flew by. This time the man chose only to sit and watch. He did not cling to the beauty and grace of the bird. Nor did he cling to any desire to possess that beauty and grace. He chose not to waste time chasing the bird but instead decided to take the time to enjoy it. He observed the change from which the bird was arising, and he experienced the beauty and the grace of the bird in flight."

"Thusly the man discovered that there was no beauty and grace, there was only change. Change that gave birth to the moment to moment rising and falling of the birds wings. With this realization he continued to watch the bird until it was no longer visible."

"The man realized that when the bird flew into this transitory moment, he had to allow the bird merely to be a bird, so he could experience the bird fully. By allowing the bird to enter freely into his field of vision and leave the same way, he experienced the bird on its terms, not his. In the absence of clinging to the bird, the man experienced this bird of change instead of missing it completely as he had before, blinded from it by his own desire. He no longer engaged in a selfish struggle to possess that which he couldn't keep from changing. Instead, he participated in this moment of change without trying to cling to it, and he became a full participant in life."

For the first time in my life I was feeling connected to all the things around me. With so much around me, nurturing my life, I will never be alone again. On another occasion I sat and looked at all of the wonderful shades overhead as they sat in living color. The park had so many trees so close together that the colors would change quickly from red to yellow to green to orange as I moved my eyes across the row. I got the image in my mind of an artist splashing his paints across a blank canvas, like the ones I had seen many times on public television. Through this analogy the image before me suddenly took on a whole new meaning. I recalled discovering how much adding my own values and expectations to my experience served to skew how things actually were. It now seemed that life was more or less a blank canvas until something was added to it. These trees had been splashed with a rainbow of color, which was part of the tree. The sky bathed in a cool shade of blue. What else I wondered, was blank before I added something to it? It was clear that I added something to everything in my life and not always something positive. Within myself I had an entire painter's palette of bright and dingy colors that I had splashed on the canvas of my experience of life. But I would no longer foolishly and impulsively splash my life with the dark, gloomy paints of depression and fear. I had a whole palette to choose from. So now it was time to begin the masterpiece that was to become my life.

Life was becoming brighter and brighter as I put faith in life to be my teacher instead of trying to have it all figured out all the time. In school I was taught that it was important to be right. You were always praised by the teacher for being right. In classroom discussions it was always important to ask the right questions and have the right answers. This often caused a fear of being wrong. You were always censured and laughed at in class for being wrong. I was now beginning to see the strength and value in wrongness, or more precisely, in never trying to be always right.

F.E.A.R.

Through my experience with illness and looking back on what I had been taught about being right, I discovered that F.E.A.R. stands for "favoring evidence against results." Which means, we experience this emotion called fear when we are focusing on all the evidence that suggests our efforts will result in a negative outcome instead of the one we want. A fear of proceeding because you're afraid of not getting something you want is as foolish as not walking for fear you might fall. You put more weight on your worry that the outcome will be unfavorable, and favor it over the potential gains of the desired outcome. How silly is that?

We learn that being wrong is dangerous and not part of the learning process but more a reflection of unpreparedness or inability. Not having all the answers needs to be recognized as a process of elimination until the only answer we're left with will point us in the direction we need to go. This makes more sense than frustrating ourselves into stopping before we begin.

I now actively seek out opportunities to get all misperceptions out of my head by asking questions. My focus isn't on whether I will appear ignorant; my focus is on learning something, and if I have a question, I will find the answer. I will stumble, and I may be laughed at or chastised by the ignorant and insecure while in my pursuit of knowledge. But always remember: there is no goal worth reaching that doesn't leave you postmarked from the journey to reach it. There will be struggle, uncertainty and frustration. But so what? Everyday life is the same way, and we're managing that.

Please Visit www.BrianRKing.com

Fear should be reserved for two things: fight or flight. Fear is a survival instinct that serves us well. Disappointment or not always being right is not life threatening. Why fear it? When we fear those things that threaten our ego, we value security over success. Fear of disappointment is a tumor. If you want to reach your goals, you have to fall and scrape up your knees up a few times. This is the art of learning to walk. A bird may be born to fly but that doesn't mean it has to get it right the first time.

After the loss of my friendships as well as my various illusions about life, I furiously punished myself because my perceptions had been wrong, when for so long, the facts had taught me I was right. Needing to be right all of the time is a tumor the cure is seeking to do what's right now. The more I became acquainted with the ever-changing state of affairs around me, I came to realize that there was no right—there was only right now. I began to use this as my barometer as it was proving to be far more reliable than anything I'd encountered so far. Each moment of life clearly had its own issues to be resolved, and that would determine what was right now. I think I'm better off paying attention to what is right now and being a part of that. I'm finding it to be right more often than I am.

I spent too much time in my life, as have many folks I know, burying myself in self-doubt and insecurity and never going out of my way to breathe in as much life as possible. Unfortunately, it took almost losing my life for me to discover that if I want anything in life, I have to act and act now. The house is burning, and you have to get out. If you don't, you will suffer the consequences of your stubbornness and inaction.

As I became more in touch with how I had been responsible for the way I dealt with my illness, I accepted the tumors I was creating. I began reflecting more on how I had traveled through life up to this point. Having ignored what was right now for so long, I wondered how many times I had done more harm than good when my own will was my only consideration.

Marking My Path

One day after a heavy rain, which seemed to clear up as quickly as it arose, I took another walk to the park. The ground was very soft, and I noticed how my feet were sinking into the ground leaving an obvious trace of where I had been. I was leaving an obvious mark as I traveled. I began to think again about the mark I had left as I walked through life because of the ideas and attitudes I had kept for so long. Unlike physical cancers, cancers of the mind are contagious. I wondered what I had been spreading. With this in mind, I contemplated the path I must begin to walk to correct and improve upon it, to exact a cure. There has been enough suffering in my life, and I was through causing it in the lives of others. My Hara was now pointing in a new direction. One there is no turning back from.

"Walk a path in its center, and its edges will not blunt. I need to stay centered and balanced. When I lose focus, I stumble and cut my feet on the edges. If doubts or the hurtful influence of the world around me consistently distract me, my path will adopt these distracting characteristics as I veer off course. I must keep my eyes pointed in the direction I intend to go, not to the left nor to the right, and never looking back."

"If I walk my path with my head bowed in shame and the subsequent weight on my toes digs the walk of shame into my path, wherever I walk, shame walks with me. If I hold my nose upward with pride, the weight on my heels, stain my path with pride as well as the paths of those I cross. As I lean toward one extreme it creates physical and spiritual imbalance. Such extremes serve to corrupt and damage my ability to be flexible and adjust where needed."

"I lose my balance forward in shame. I lose my balance backward with pride. Either way it is easier to knock me down because life requires balance, not imbalance, of extremes. A walk of haste and impatience scares my path with the constant pushing off of my feet. A walk of sadness scares my path as my feet drag along. A walk of anger dents my path as my feet stomp along. A walk of procrastination gives a sag to my path as the weight of my feet remains too long in one place."

"Walking my path in any extreme way will distort its original nature. Thus by continuing in such a way, there may come a point at which there is no spot on the path that gives hint to my original nature. My nature may then be impossible to recover. Thus by remaining centered in my true nature, no mark will be left."

"Without haste I make no step before the previous step is complete. Without haste there is no loss of balance, and there is no hesitation in my step. My step may then be placed with even weight. Weight placed with care and not haste will not scratch the uncorrupted path but only provide a soft nurturing touch."

"I will take my time and not begin a new task before the previous one is finished. What kind of a future will I have if I don't do the best I can in the present?" Less and less I put a sense of importance on my selfish wants. For it was more obvious than ever that what I wanted did not hold the same importance as what was needed in a particular situation. For example, I may have gotten angry when it rained because my plans had been spoiled as a result. But some farmers may have needed those rains so their crops could grow and their families could have money to put food on their own tables. The animals may have needed it to avoid dehydration. The trees may have needed it to grow and produce oxygen so I could breathe and live. So, which is really more important, my trivial plans or the rain? Now when it rains, I can't help but smile."

So many things surround us, each with their own set of needs and wants. I will never be so arrogant as to assume I know what things are most important in life, because although I am a part of it, I didn't design it. But what I can do is watch the things that are responsible for creating this life, and by watching what they do, I can learn what is most needed and which methods are most successful. The very world we live in sustains us as we strive for success; we cannot be gluttonous as we proceed. In being so we deplete the very forces that we rely on to sustain us in our journey, and before long, they will not be able to hold us up anymore. Take care of and give each situation what it needs, then move on to what you need. Support all those around you, and the more you support them the more they will support you. Although my friends left me in my time of need, I now go out of my way to support as many people as I can. It can be something as small as a smile or a kind word, but still I'm supporting them. I have no doubt that the support will be there when I need it.

I am now taking full responsibility for the impact I make on those around me. Taking full responsibility is a cure for blame. I know that as part of the wondrous variety in life, I could either help it or hurt it. I find that things accomplish more and function better when they cooperate instead of competing.

Think about what a life without variety would be like. Life is change. Without variety, life could not happen. If there was only one custom or method, one direction or design, one color, one scent, only one single option, then what could change change into? Without variety, it could do nothing. Imagine a machine in a factory with rotating cogs, joined by interlocking teeth. If every cog suddenly rotated clockwise, they would not move. They would all lock up, as they competed, against each other for movement. Without alternating rotation, without variety of rotation, no movement, no function can take place.

If every organ in the human body were only useful for the exact same function, then we would not survive. Each organ has its own specific shape and its own specific function. Through this wonderful variety of interaction, this interdependent function, a living being is able to sustain itself.

The more I learn, the more I have yet to learn. Now I can see a life more intricate and more vast than before. It's amazing what lies before me now that I realize there is more to life than what goes on between my ears. The more I watch and learn from nature, the less I worry. No matter what problems I have in life, everything still seems to be taken care of. The sun rises and sets, and the world keeps on turning. I realize that I'm but one piece of the great puzzle of life. I am not responsible for the whole puzzle but only for what my piece provides toward maintaining the stability of the whole. I don't have to worry about controlling so much of my life because I never had control in the first place; I only had a desire for it. I couldn't control my birth; I can't prevent my death. I can't change the weather or the actions of others, because these things are none of my business and out of my hands. Things are always in a state of perpetual change, moving in the same direction. The moment I grab for something I wish to control, it has already changed and slipped right through my fingers. I can't presume to guide the destiny of things I have no hand in. There are only two things that I can think of that are any of my business to control: who I am and what I do. Who I allow myself to be and the actions I choose as an expression of that is where my responsibility lies. Although I am only one piece of the puzzle, this carries tremendous responsibility. No one but me can determine what my actions will be. There is no one to blame for the conclusions I draw, the choices I make and the actions I take.

Understanding this has far-reaching consequences. With no room to make excuses, thoughtfulness is essential. In all of my relationships, I can choose and am responsible for everything I bring to each relationship. I can decide to increase the suffering in life with what I bring or I can choose to reduce it. It's my choice what I give to this life and only my responsibility to live it. No one can make me do anything. I can only choose to.

I was responsible for how I felt when my friends left me, and I was responsible for how I reacted. At the time I blamed them for how I felt. I was caught up in the "they made me do it" logic. The reason my emotional pain didn't go away during that time was because I was placing the blame for a problem when the responsibility was mine. I was essentially waiting around for someone else to come along and solve my problems. It was like spraying water on the smoke to put out the fire. Now I have learned to take responsibility for myself. There is tremendous freedom in taking responsibility for myself. In taking charge, peer pressure isn't a factor because I realize that any choice I make is my own. If I only take responsibility for myself and am always true to myself, I will always be myself. No longer is my mind filled with the blame of holding others responsible for my life or the guilt of having let others talk me into something I now regret.

Being Myself

In fact, by being true to myself and thus just being myself, I am left to act with deeper conviction and confidence. Since I and I alone am responsible for how I choose to behave, if I choose to treat people well, then nothing they do should change that. If I am kind to someone and they treat me like garbage, then I made my choice of what I would bring to that situation and they made theirs. In the past I may have gotten angry with them because I would have felt I deserved to be treated nicely, too. But I cannot make someone else's decisions for them. If I choose to be pleasant, there is no reason why I should be talked out of it. But it is important to respect the other person's responsibility to make their choice.

Please Visit www.BrianRKing.com

As I continue to watch and learn, I gain a greater awareness of just how much is contributed to life because things are just being themselves and taking responsibility for being so. I observe how the sun warms the earth because it is just being responsible for being the sun, which is the same for the tree, the ocean and even me. How much could I give to this life by just being myself? It's inspiring to see what power lies in doing something so simple.

In thinking about what being myself meant, I was able to resolve an issue that still lingered in the back of my mind: the issue that arose from having only one testicle—the feeling of being incomplete. I felt a little freakish with my bald head and perceived inadequacies. But as I discovered the wonder of variety and the strength that comes with that variety, my insecurities diminished. I discovered that who I was as a person and as a man came from being the man I am. I had to contribute my unique brand of masculinity and humanity to this world whatever form it came in. It wasn't my responsibility to be the definition of masculinity I had come to know. One testicle or five, I was still myself and that defined my value not the packaging I was presently dressed in but the value of its contents.

A few days later a young lady I knew was having a bad self-esteem day. She expressed her dissatisfaction with herself by listing a handful of reasons why her body was inadequate: "I'm too short. I wear glasses. I'm not pretty enough, etc." I recalled how I struggled with similar feelings of inadequacy. I went to the young lady and offered her an analogy that seemed to make all the difference to her.

"Suppose you have a diamond, that is beautiful and unique, second to none. It will always simply be itself and never otherwise. This diamond cannot be scratched or cracked or harmed in anyway. It has near indomitable integrity. If I ever tried to color it, this would only serve as decoration. Whatever exterior changes you make to it, it is still a diamond."

"If it were wrapped in expensive packaging or even with simple and crumpled paper it is still a diamond wrapped inside. If I placed it inside a short container or a box that's six feet tall, if I dropped it in a box ten feet wide or in a thin box it wouldn't matter for a single moment. For the wrapping can never tell what treasures lie inside."

"The diamond is not its package, so how it is wrapped does not reveal its intrinsic value. You must look inside for that. I find the same is true for me, for you and for anyone else I meet."

How wonderful to take responsibility for who and what I am. I mentioned before that I was now taking responsibility for everything I brought to the relationships in my life. The more I thought about this, the more I thought about the kind of friend I could be to others by simply giving what I could. My friends had left me when I was in need. That was their choice. At this point I made a promise to myself that if I ever had the opportunity to reduce the suffering in someone else's life, I would not pass it up. That is my choice. I began to write about the kind of friend that I thought I could be.

"I am like a lighthouse keeping watch over the ships at sea. I shine my light upon them should they encounter adversity. When the waters beneath them are churning and tossing them about, I cast my beam upon them to assist them until things become calm again."

"I will keep my light upon them so they'll always know I'm there. This struggle on the rugged sea is shared by us both. When the path ahead is clouded by a dense and dangerous fog, I'll guide you to a clearing and through all of the turmoil."

"I'll keep you safe from harm as you approach the rocky shore. When you venture upon your journey and adverse conditions begin, I'll lead you through the waters so you can safely dock. The moment you need a guiding light, I will be there again."

I could have used a friend like that. So now I am determined to be a friend like that. Although it's always preferable to get what you give, I have stated many times that that is not what occurred in my situation. I now give because I choose to, not because I expect a return.

My life is becoming more simplified. As I gradually relinquish my obsession with the past, I realize more what is my business and let go of what isn't. By doing this, life becomes more manageable. Like the tree, I live more in the present. I take life one moment at a time, mostly because that's the only way it comes. It's amazing how when you handle life the way it's dished out, it is much more manageable and less stressful.

When I was going through my experience with cancer, I enveloped myself in the entirety of all of my wants and fears. I don't remember once taking things one moment at a time. Instead I would long for the past and wish for or fear the future instead of tending to the present. The best way I can describe how I went from worrying about everything at once and learning to take life one moment at a time, in addition to the bending of the tree, lies in the process of assembling a puzzle.

Life is a giant puzzle, but an immensely manageable one. And we all contribute a valuable piece. As each new day passes and I come more to terms with what happened and what it all means to me, I feel the pain of my ordeal fade further and further away. I was raised to believe that pain and its expression was a sign of weakness and was essentially the enemy of strength and good character. It was a long time before I saw my pain clearly enough to realize that it could be used as a source of healing.

A Crack in the Soil

I watched my grandfather harvest his small garden the summer after my chemo ended. As he would tear the roots from the ground, a small hole would remain where life had once flourished. But the next year he would be planting new seeds in those same holes so life could begin anew. This was another lesson I was slowly beginning to learn. Each hole that was dug in my spirit with every loss I endured, could now support a new bud of life sprouting where a seed of hope was planted. It may be a sign of strength to endure pain by not showing it, but it's also equally, if not more valuable, to endure pain while learning and growing from it.

I began seeing the earth and soil in a new way. During the summer I would notice it all dried out from drought, pale and riddled with cracks. It appeared to be breaking from the dryness of the heat. It seemed to be opening itself up, becoming more vulnerable, weakening. Or was this a sign of its strength?

In opening wide to the coming rains, the cracks allow the soil to be thoroughly filled will water. It would appear that opening myself up would allow me to be nourished and filled with what I need as well. If I close myself in fear that I might be hurt, then I am likely to shut out that which might help me grow.

This is more an example of the soils' strength than vulnerability. It allows itself the help it needs for continued vitality. The soil regains its consistency, its strength and its fertility through its openness.

The soil also allows seeds to enter it. Then before you know it, within this vulnerability a seed was planted, and now life begins to grow. I know now what appears as inadequacy when I experience vulnerability, is an opening in which life can begin, when I let the seeds of growth come in.

I'm filled with soil, potential and an endless number of openings from which new growth can sprout. Like my grandfather's garden, I need only to allow in the seeds that will help me grow. I'm already looking for them, and I won't stop as they are only limited by my desire to find them.

One of the hardest lessons to swallow throughout all of this was not only learning to trust enough to allow hope to take root, but also to realize that there is a time when I must let go of the past and the things I loved there. Although the losses I suffered were great, had I not endured them, I wouldn't have the quality of life I do now. I would not be the man I am today.

As I watch the things in my everyday life pass and go the way of all things, I realize that there is nothing in life that I can ever have. I can only have the experience of these things. I now understand that everything passes, nothing stays the same. Everything is temporary. So what is it that I thought I had? I began to realize that the things I suffered the greatest sense of loss from, were the things I thought were mine, including my friends, my girlfriend and my life. How silly was I to think I owned something that I couldn't keep? Everything I had experienced was simply that: a passing experience. Since everything passes, everything is eventually taken away. So obviously there was nothing that was there to be possessed. But there was and is plenty to be experienced.

I understood now that the more I grasped for the things that could not be held, the more that it hurt when they passed. This brought me back to the knowledge that there will only be two things in life I will ever have: who I am and what I do. These two things can only be exercised when given a life as a vehicle to practice them. A life which, of course, is on its way out. I had believed that I had lost a life that was never mine in the first place. It was but a moment in time. A moment I wasted because I didn't see it for what it was and didn't appreciate it when I could. For that reason, I missed it horribly when it was gone.

The secret to enjoying something was not in having it, but by experiencing it when I could. Whether it is a car, a sunset, a relationship with a loved one or the very life I live. When it does finally pass, I will hopefully not suffer as much as I would have, had I expected it to stay.

I have no possessions, therefore I have nothing to lose. I only have this time, which is also passing. So I will do all I can not to waste it. As I said before, the more I learn, the more I have left to learn. I will never be an expert in this life because my life is a work in progress, an evolving work that requires patience, diligence and an eye for detail. I will carry on as a perpetual student. For with every passing breath, I learn more about myself and what life has in store for me. Experience has always been the greatest teacher. My life is the greatest reward. As I continue on my journey, I will do so as a dedicated and eager student of life. I leave this section of the book with the oath I follow as I learn: I will always remember to learn and grow and never be corrupted by what I think I know.

PART TWO

A CURE FOR WHAT AILS YOU

Walking the path of life successfully
begins with a simple technique.
Put one foot in front of the other,
and do it with confidence.

CHAPTER THREE

The Responsibility Cure

What you've been reading so far was only meant to tweak your brain and prepare you for the work to be done. So do you feel primed? It is now time to get down to business and start putting the cure to work. The rest of this book is a series of techniques and observations that will lead you through the process of how to begin to embody the ideas that have led to my own sense of self-mastery and my ability to succeed in life by curing the psychological cancers that I put in my own way.

Before you read further, you may want to ask yourself the same question that I did. In the story of your life, are you a victim or a victor? Choose quickly because the story of you as a victor begins now.

Reinhold Neibuhr wrote, "Grant me the serenity to accept the things I cannot change, courage to change the things I can, and wisdom to know the difference." Although I haven't been on this planet very long, as you've read by now, I have acquired a lot of mileage. I believe I can address the desire to learn to accept the things you cannot change, identify the things you can change (the courage to change them is up to you) and begin to understand the difference.

As I touched on earlier, I've learned that all I can really count on is the present. I contemplated for some time how my life was seemingly out of control and how I couldn't determine what, if any, kind of control I had over my circumstances. When I began looking to myself for what I could do about exacting the change I wanted, it finally hit me. I realized that I possessed total control over two things, control that couldn't be taken from me by any external means, no matter what my circumstances. These two things involve the areas of my life where I previously thought I had no control. But by taking responsibility for these two things, I was able to regain control over my life in spite of its unpredictable and chaotic nature. I was able to establish a sense of order when the world around me appeared to have none. This realization is encompassed in what I call "The Two Responsibilities," which I mentioned in passing earlier but will discuss in detail now.

Referring back to Mr. Neibuhr's statement, these two responsibilities are the things that I can change and can control. All other things then are the things I cannot change. As you read and embrace the concepts I will share with you, you will begin to acquire the wisdom to know the difference between the two. There are several ideas I'll share that will help you accept the things you cannot change more easily. We will begin with a little exercise.

Taking Responsibility and Taking Control

On the lines provided below, list a maximum of ten of your responsibilities in life.

1._____
2._____
3._____
4._____
5._____
6._____
7._____
8._____
9._____
10._____

Now that your list is completed, ask yourself the following questions: How many did you list?

How many of the responsibilities involve meeting the expectations of other people?

How many of the responsibilities require the cooperation of factors that are out of your control?

How many of the responsibilities could be difficult to carry out because of interference from factors out of your control?

Review your list carefully, and choose the one responsibility that causes you the greatest amount of stress (mental, physical and/or emotional discomfort) and difficulty. Which responsibility seems to be the greatest cancer in your life, the one that depletes your energy and is harmful to you? Keep this responsibility in mind as we proceed. Since this responsibility causes you the most difficulty, applying these concepts to it should make it easier to apply them to less complicated tasks.

Referring back to the previous list of questions, I would suggest to you that all of your responsibilities contain some elements that are out of your control. In fact, accomplishing even the smallest tasks throughout our day is dependent upon factors we take for granted and elements that we can do nothing about. For example, my ability to complete the morning routine that prepares me for the day depends upon the presence of running water, the electricity being on, having clothes to wear, food to eat, etc. Stress begins with our awareness of and attitude toward the uncontrollable aspects of our lives. How much of your day do you think is spent fretting over unfulfilled responsibilities that were derailed by things you couldn't control even if you wanted to or worrying about the effects of things in general that you can't control?

Please Visit www.BrianRKing.com

So many people I know suffer from "control cancer." They want control over anything and everything and practically give themselves ulcers in their pursuit of controlling things that are either out of their control or simply none of their business. Control cancer leads to "responsibility cancer," which is when people hold themselves responsible for the world's woes and thus take on the problems of others as their own. The main problems with responsibility cancer are that we cannot solve other people's problems for them no matter how hard we work at it nor do we allow ourselves any time to deal with our own. This unachievable goal of global caretaker eats away at us as this inflated sense of responsibility we've created for ourselves becomes so overwhelming that it consumes us, our lives and begins wearing us down. There is a cure for the control and responsibility cancers that we choose to grow within ourselves, however.

One way control cancer eats away at us is when something doesn't get done or doesn't go right. We then get mad at it for not going our way or become angry at ourselves for not having more control where we think we should. We are often personally offended when the world doesn't operate at our discretion. For example, when you're in a hurry in your car because you have a responsibility to get somewhere at a certain time, and a red light catches you, what are you mad at? You're mad at the light because it interfered with your progress, right? Why? It has nothing to do with you, it's not personal and it's something you can't do anything about. Nonetheless, our minds begin spinning with a stress-inducing internal dialogue about what the red light means in the course of our progress. Comments such as "Almost made it" leaves one feeling like the light beat you in some kind of competition. "Darn it, I was making good time." This puts the light in the role of being an enemy in your effort to accomplish your goals, as though the red light was some personal insult to your schedule. This is just one small example of how we relate to the uncontrollables in our lives can determine the quality of our day and the amount of stress in it.

This kind of thinking is also what resulted in my anger toward my friends for not treating me the way I expected them to when I had cancer. It is the cancerous thinking that states everything has to go my way for my benefit at all times or something is terribly wrong with the world. As absurd as this thinking is, we still do it. Some of us do it some of the time, others most of the time. Take an inventory of all of your reactions today, and see how many of them stem from control or responsibility cancer.

Your Locus of Control

There are many assumptions or expectations we might bring into our dealings with the countless uncontrollables of our everyday life. Often assumptions can vary from person to person since our internal dialogue or self-talk varies. These assumptions arise in part from the perception that experiences arise from events outside of ourselves and thus happen to us. This is referred to as an "external locus of control," which means you perceive that forces outside of yourself influence and control your life. This is the belief that your circumstances are bigger than you are and control your responses. Let's see if we can begin to think about this a new way.

First of all, nothing is ever outside of ourselves if it is anything that concerns us. As soon as we react to something, it is inside us. It has entered our experience, and we undergo a change as a result of our processing of it. Whether it is the red light we took in, a warm breeze, a kind word or a not so kind word, nothing that catches our attention happens outside of us. In other words, things don't happen to us; what we do with them happens to us. Our experiences and the lessons of our lives result from what we do with what we take in to ourselves. Therefore, experiences are actually the outcomes of our responses to events, and we can do whatever we wish with them.

The person who takes full responsibility for their own experiences has an "internal locus of control," which is the realization that they may not control the events of their lives but they do control their responses to them. The easiest way to demonstrate how the internal locus of control works is by using an equation I learned from one of my mentors, Jack Canfield. The equation states that E + R = O. There are "E"vents in your life and your "R"esponses to them, which equal the "O"utcomes you experience as a result of your responses to the events (Canfield, 2000). You can use this equation to gauge your responses in any situation.

When I was sick, I clearly had an external locus of control. I believed that my anger and depression was everybody else's fault because of how they were treating me. How cancerous is that thinking? But when I began to understand that my feelings were the outcomes of my responses to how they were treating me, I took responsibility for them and acquired an internal locus of control. When you realize this, you also realize that your circumstances are never bigger than you are. You may not be able to control what happens around you, but you can control what happens inside you.

Not only can you choose the response you will have, but in doing so, you can actually change the outcome. Think of the E + R = O equation in terms of 2 + 2 = 4. If you can't change the event, you can change your response and thus change the outcome. If you always respond the same way to the same event, you will experience the same outcome. So, 2 + 2 will always equal 4. But if you change your response you change the outcome. So now your equation might read 2 + 3 = 5 (Canfield, 2000). Simple, huh? In the bigger scheme of things, you can literally change your life simply by changing your mind. You've just learned part of the "responsibility cure," but there is more to come.

As I mentioned earlier, when the responsibility and control cancers consume us, the things we actually do have control over tend to be the things we expend the least amount of energy on maximizing. But that can all change right now. What if you could construct your life so that every responsibility you had contained only the factors that were totally in your control? You'd no longer stress about the other things, and life would be simpler and less stressful. Believe it or not, there are responsibilities like this.

Refer back to your list of responsibilities at the beginning of this exercise. In spite of the numerous amount of responsibilities you may have listed I am going to suggest that there are only two responsibilities you are capable of following through on consistently. And I'll bet neither of them appears on your list. If my suggestion is accurate, these responsibilities are the only two you will ever need to accomplish day to day, the only responsibilities you have the ability and control to accomplish. And because these two responsibilities exist in every activity of your life, you can have total control when it comes to fulfilling them.

These two responsibilities emerge from and are nurtured by your Hara, the foundation of who you are. If you can master these two responsibilities, your ability to focus on where you can be most effective in any situation will open like a floodgate. Here we go.

Your Responsibilities

The two things in life you are responsible for are *who you are* and *what you do*. Before you read on, you need to make a personal commitment to take 100% responsibility for these areas of your life. No doubts, no reservations, no excuses. Unless you take these responsibilities in your hands, the rest will be next to impossible to accomplish. Did you commit? Are you ready? Okay keep going.

Who you are refers to your Self:

• Your cognitive wiring, your programming

• All of your beliefs, values and attitudes

• Perceptions, assumptions, expectations about yourself and others

- The "R" in your E + R = O
- All other impressions that guide and inspire your navigation through this life

What you do refers to your Actions:

- The things you say to yourself as you cognitively process your experience, what you do as a result of your "R"esponses
- Your behavior, the outcomes you help create

Remember, you can pick and choose your beliefs, indulge in whatever attitude you like. These two responsibilities are the foundation of your internal locus of control, because you feel and are in control when you take control where you have it.

Who you are is best expressed in what you say to yourself, also referred to as the "internal critic." It expresses what you think you're worth, or how you describe yourself to yourself and others. Does the critic impose limits, or congratulate you on a job well done?

Your two responsibilities are at the heart of your being; they are fueled by your Hara. So if who you are is more of a critic than a support to yourself, then this is the energy that fuels the direction your life takes. Your cancerous critic takes the energy that can be used for progress and uses it to fuel doubt and discouragement. Think of it as buying a car that only turns left. You've chosen to invest in a vehicle that limits where you can go in life.

If you insist on being a critic, be a critical success. Remember the discussion we had earlier about thinking from your Hara? I hope it is evident that the description I've provided for who you are stems from those processes enjoyed by the brain, in that the brain takes the lead in all cases. I'd be surprised if I met a person who claimed that relying on his or her brain didn't get them in trouble regularly.

Again, I point out that learning to be guided by your Hara will create an increased tendency toward certainty in your decision-making. When you work from your Hara, the only motivation you need to follow through on your decision is the strength of your commitment to that decision. Remember that your Hara is your source of balance. Your Hara prefers balance—that is why you get the queasy feeling in a situation that your brain might be telling you is okay, but your gut is warning you against. Your brain lacks the sensitivity your Hara has.

Important note: the queasiness I'm talking about here is not the butterflies you feel when your brain is engaged in nervous self-talk that is causing you to worry. If that's where the queasiness is coming from, then there is usually no other danger than that which you create for yourself. The queasiness I am talking about is that early warning sign of danger or that gut feeling that tells you you're doing the right thing. I've been in a few traffic accidents where my Hara tightened up a few seconds before I was hit, and I had no idea the hit was coming. You can also experience a tightness in your Hara that pushes you to act in a positive direction. I've heard people who run into burning houses to help people escape describe a tingling in their bellies that pulled them toward the house. This is the Hara telling you your actions will have a safe outcome.

To assist you in letting go of the hold your *who you are* programming has on you, it is important to realize that beliefs are inherently disposable; the programming that makes you you is a work in progress, undergoing constant revision and transformation at your discretion. John C. Lilly said that "Every belief is a limit to be examined and transcended (Canfield, 2000)." Moshe Feldenkrais also recognized that "The only thing permanent about our behavior patterns is our belief that they are so (Canfield, 2000)."

Remember, limiting beliefs are detrimental to us, one of the worst of all being the belief that we have limits. If this were true, we'd be capable of so little growth that we'd proceed through life virtually unchanged.

The truth of the matter is that none of us is the same way we were the day we left our mother's womb. We have all undergone a substantial change process and continue to do so. The butterfly may undergo the transformation process only once, but we can do it daily or moment to moment to whatever degree we choose. As we encounter new experiences, information and acquire education, who we are results from these opportunities for revision and refinement.

Consider your life a story that is always being written and rewritten, with new characters entering and leaving the story daily. In a way, your beliefs are characters in your story. They guide the action by setting the rule for how you as the main character will proceed. Your decisions about what to believe determines what has meaning and what you consider trivial. A simple example of this would be if you believe that people who call you names are bad or mean. You feel this way because you believe that there are such things called insults and that they are to be perceived as negative. This also says something about the responses you choose to the comments of others. You've essentially programmed yourself to be offended.

An alternative belief would be that statements made by others are opinions, based solely on the rules of their story. Just because somebody throws something at you doesn't mean you have to catch it. You can decide how or even whether to invest yourself in another person's words or actions.

As I said, like any character in a story your beliefs will come and go. Growth is a result of adjustments to changes in your circumstances. Growth in plants results from its response to the presence of water and sunlight. We grow from the presence of positive forces in our lives or other experiences that force us to make adjustments.

Beliefs are characters that come in and out; they can also be seen as tools used by you—the master carpenter for shaping your reality into the work of art you envision for yourself. As such, they should only be tools you can use to accomplish your goals. More importantly, you need to be in control of your tools—not the other way around. If your beliefs/tools control you, especially when that control results in a negative outcome, then it's time to throw them out and replace them with tools you can use. Tools can also become old, blunted, worn out or in all other ways not as effective as they used to be for meeting the challenge. So if you can't use it, lose it. If you weigh yourself down with a lot of stuff that is of no use, then what do you become? I don't recall a time in my life when clutter has ever been to my advantage.

You choose your tools, you write the story, you decide what to splash on the canvas that makes you who you are and your actions are a direct result of that. So, clearly who you are and what you do are your responsibilities alone. This is the time when people usually bring up all the excuses they can as to why their parents or any other person are actually responsible for the way they are. My all-purpose response to that assertion is that your parents are responsible for the causes or events they contributed to your life, but you are responsible for the effect or responses. As children we usually lack the self-awareness to process what is happening around us or our reactions to it. But once we are aware, we hold all of the cards and all of the responsibility for changing the outcome or keeping it the same. At this point, excuses lack any credibility. Whatever judgement you may make regarding your experiences, how you process them and what you give back to the world in response lies squarely on your shoulders.

In spite of what we are used to thinking, our beliefs and attitudes are no more who we are than a carpenter is his tools or a dancer is her feet. It is how we utilize these things that makes us who we are. Who we are, as I said earlier, is a work in progress. Our lives can only become whatever our current beliefs or attitudes allow us to conceive for ourselves.

A carpenter's tools may become lost or broken, but an artist and the art never die. Beethoven wasn't hampered by his deafness because the art survived within him. An artist with the most refined skills is not an artist if she has nothing within her to express. Who I am as a man has nothing to do with how many testicles I have. My masculinity is not wrapped up in my tool, so to speak. Don't hold so tightly to your thoughts, theories and beliefs, because they change and grow as readily as you do. They are instruments that guide us, like a steering wheel guides a car. We are not our beliefs and the car is not the road. What matters is our willingness to adjust as the road changes. When we mistake our beliefs for who we are, we close the door to growth. We mistake our cocoon for the world, not considering the option of leaving it. It's time to break out.

By choosing to embrace this new thinking, you'll have to give up a few things like blaming other people or other things for your thoughts and reactions. No longer can you say "that makes me mad;" what actually occurred was you got mad, you chose that response. The "they made me do it" defense is a thing of the past. The processing and the emotional response to an event result from the value or meaning you place on the experience and are, therefore, completely your doing. In other words, you're choosing to engage in the activity of anger, sadness, etc, in response to an event. You weren't given anger by something; you're giving anger to it.

Giving Your Mind Away

Assigning blame or responsibility to others for the things you have control over is something I call "giving your mind away." This is something we do quite readily and far too often. Giving your mind away means giving control of yourself over to others. This applies mostly to allowing others to manipulate our thoughts and emotions. I spent 18 years of my life doing this, indulging in programmed responses to behaviors whose meanings I never questioned. We give power to others over our emotions, allowing our hearts to become their personal gymnasiums to play whatever games they like. The more of your mind you give away, the less of yourself there is for you to use to reach your goals, because you give someone else too many of the strings to pull.

In addition, when we look primarily to others to tell us what to think and believe, and we swallow it without any examination, some might consider this a sign of trust in that person; I consider it careless. If that person's word is all you have to go on, then you walk around being guided by a belief that has no foundation. As you know, something built without a foundation doesn't stand very long. "So and so said it was true," is not a good reason to believe something. Not to mention, if this person is the only source of that belief, then you must run to them for their counsel, and they determine when the belief should be adjusted. Of course, it is important to seek the guidance of others in matters you're unfamiliar with. But when it comes to your two responsibilities, don't give power to someone else, especially over the only two areas of your life where you have complete control. These responsibilities need to be held sacred to you because they define you as well as what you're able to give to others. The more control over yourself you give away, the less you have of yourself to give to others.

I understand how easy it is to have your mind taken from you by the millions of distractions we face every day. Later in the book when you practice the exercise called "Minding the Breath," you'll learn to be able to tell when your mind is leaving you. When your mind wanders and becomes distracted, your task is to get it back. Whenever you feel overwhelmed and out of control, your goal is to stay in control of yourself; self-control is the only real control you can ever have. As you read, I will introduce to you ways in which increasing self-control and thus control of your life direction is done.

The Search for Security

One of the biggest thieves of our mind is our endless search for security in life. We seek comfort, safety and certainty in all walks of life. The problem here is that we strive for something that doesn't exist. In other words "If it can be taken from you, it isn't yours." I don't speak merely of material things but of living things as well. My life clearly isn't mine—I didn't create it, and I don't know when it will end, but I do bear the responsibility for what I do and create with it. My wife is not mine, although we entered into an agreement that we will be by each other's side forever. I will lose her someday, whether it be "till death do us part" or some other reason, so I can never be complacent when it comes to enjoying and valuing what is currently available for my enjoyment.

This search for security is the root of human suffering as far as I can tell. This search drives us to try and hold on to that which we want or to avoid that which we don't want. Besides our two responsibilities, everything can be taken from us. No matter how much we care for it or struggle with it, it will leave. The main reason we experience loss in life is because we come to count on something's continued presence for our well-being, which is an unreasonable expectation. Things move in and out of our lives and we need to understand their impermanence if we are to benefit from their presence while we have them.

Trying to avoid that which we don't want is foolish as well. Once I was diagnosed with cancer, I could not want it with all my heart. The not wanting what was unavoidable could only serve to increase my suffering, and it certainly did. What was the lesson we learned earlier? If you can't change the event, then change your response to it. One of my best friends is always stating how she doesn't deal well with change. When I hear this from her or anyone else, I am amazed by what a blatant misattribution it is of the real issue. Change isn't the problem; it is effortless. It's happening this moment on a massive scale. What they have a problem with is the reminder that security is a no show in the game of life. When their security is threatened, they blame change instead of realizing that it is their own expectations that are problematic.

Therefore, our continued aversion to the reminder that security based on the idea of permanence catapults us into a self-induced onslaught of physical and emotional pain as well as dozens of other trials and tribulations. We can continue to run and hide and otherwise avoid the things we don't like. But as I said, it is the avoidance of these negative things that causes us pain and suffering. When we find we can't avoid them, we feel like something is wrong with us. "Why do bad things keep happening? I'm a good person. They shouldn't happen to me." Well, why not? The person you are has more to do with how you meet the challenges in your life, not whether you have them or not.

What often happens is, the more we realize we are unable to find the security we seek, the more we slowly begin to close ourselves off, and our unwillingness to take risks causes us to shrink into a little subjective fish bowl. We fear having to try anything that might result in failure or loss, and as a result, we stick only to those things that to that point have been consistent. We do our job the same old way; we keep on having the same old day. The difference between the employer and the employee is that the employer focuses on increasing success, which is fueled by embracing change and taking risks, while the employee focuses on increasing security by reducing risks and minimizing change. So when someone asks, "What's new?" Most people respond "Nothing." Well, that's your fault. You have effectively worked yourself into a rut of complacency in order to maintain an illusion of security and certainty. Complacency is the enemy of growth. You spend all of your time doing and little or none of it being. It is time to start thinking bigger; you have to step out of the fishbowl. The person who said "the sky's the limit" wasn't thinking big enough. In my way of thinking, the sky is only the beginning. Although I wouldn't recommend it, it took a physical tumor to smash my fishbowl and put me in a situation where either I learned how to survive in an environment without the fishbowl or I suffocated and died. Obviously, I chose to learn how to breathe air again.

Let go of the favoring evidence against results (F.E.A.R.) mentality. Stop fighting to keep what you've got, lose the fear of losing anything and by all means drop the fear of striving for something more for fear of losing what you already have. Remember, nothing is yours to begin with. Whether you strive for something more or just sit on your butt, you will lose what you have anyway.

If you sit around and try to hang on to everything, you will acquire a lot—a lot of selfishness, distrust and insecurity. The trick is in giving yourself permission to let go of something you couldn't keep in the first place. This will allow you to run freely in the direction of what you want without fear of loss, because in letting go, you don't value the idea of security—you value success. Success is about taking risks and moving on, striving for new things. Security is about hanging onto what you've got and not letting go. Success continues to grow, while security and complacency stagnate. It's time to build success.

Initially I created a great deal of psychological pain for myself by clinging to the past I'd lost and resisting the change of my situation. The idea that things are permanent is cancerous to our ability to deal with change. Embracing that everything is temporary and finding comfort in that, is the cure.

Examine Your Expectations

As I mentioned earlier, our minds are routinely taken from us, mostly as a result of our own butterfingers. One of the ways is by accepting the faulty programming of others, programming that isn't designed to help us. We are often subjected to the fears and prejudices someone has created in their own minds to help further their efforts at maintaining security in their own lives. They in turn instill these thoughts in us, and these thoughts become our templates for dealing with the world. Your mind is only yours when you participate. So ask yourself, are you the puppet or the puppeteer? When you talk to yourself, who's doing the talking? Examine the rules and criticisms in your head, and determine where they came from.

Anytime you have an automatic reaction to something, like taking offense to a particular use of language or a differing viewpoint, take a brief moment, breathe and do some self-examination. Ask yourself where the threat in that statement or event was. Should others around you take responsibility for saying only the things you like? Should you be responsible for keeping others attitudes in line? I would say none of the above. Unless we decide to compile a checklist of our personal baggage to hand out to everyone so they know what will offend us, we might want to do some personal maintenance.

For starters, you need to realize that at least part of the threat lies in the challenges placed on your expectations, or shoulds. Where did you learn to respond in this way? I learned it by being raised around selfish people who always insisted on things going their way. They taught me to be selfish as well. Since I felt I never got things my way, I insisted upon it whenever I felt I had a chance to do so.

Fortunately I learned at some point that shoulds are preferences not imperatives, and I became more able to stop shoulding all over the place and learned to focus on my true responsibilities. Remember that you're responsible for who you are and what you do. Whatever anyone else chooses to contribute to the world is his or her responsibility. Your responsibility is for your contribution. We must focus solely on that which we can control and not be so preoccupied with the contributions of others. Our expectations, when not examined for their validity, can cause a great deal of difficulty.

As I said, we often get angry when things fail to turn out the way we expected them to. The reality is that we can only control two aspects of the process our two responsibilities; everything else is out of our hands. That is something you *can* expect.

Your expectations can make you intolerant as you expect that you are correct in wanting things your way. Believing yourself to be somehow more deserving of the outcome you prefer. Thus you judge and react harshly to others who seem to be doing better than you are.

Of course, your expectations lead to disappointment when you don't get what you want. You can desire and intend a particular result, but if you spend more time looking at the horizon than you do the ground your standing on, you're liable to trip and fall flat on your face.

The more you expect results from factors that you are not responsible for and not in control of, the more dissatisfied you will be. Work with what you have; acquire what you can to make what you have stronger. Wanting something you can't control is fruitless, and the pursuit of it will only increase your frustration and decrease your focus on what you can control.

Embracing your two responsibilities will bring greater peace of mind. It is comforting to go into every situation knowing what you're responsibilities are. The rest can only take care of itself. When concentrating on the two things you can control, you can execute them with complete precision and excellence, because they have your undivided attention.

Of course, simply shifting your attention from the myriad things we typically concern ourselves with to only two is not an easy task. There are several rules that people in general have acquired that prevent them from doing so. For example, here are some beliefs that many people possess in one form or another that stand in the way of this new thinking. The belief that your ability to impress people is somehow tied into your self-worth. A resoundingly common belief is that if someone doesn't treat you right, then he or she is a bad person, or even worse, there is something wrong with you. You may believe that you are entitled to anything you want and that anything less is unacceptable.

Finally, if anything bad happens in your life, then something must be wrong with you. All of these beliefs put primary importance on your expectations being met by factors that are out of your control. In addition, several of these beliefs use the reactions of others to us as a measure of the quality of our lives and ourselves. This is why these beliefs result in so much stress and disappointment. They set standards that are impossible to live up to.

So when instead we decide to be responsible for who we are and what we do, we have the final say in what we are going to contribute to life on a daily basis and what we allow it to contribute to us. If a co-worker is miserable and wants to take it out on everybody else, fine. That's what he wants to contribute. If you want to be happy and complimentary all day, that's what you want to contribute and that's your responsibility. Your attitude requires your own tenacity and commitment to follow through on it—not whether others share it or not.

I used to work in a hospital that could get very busy very quickly. This most often brought out the worst in people as they became overwhelmed and impatient. I would decide before even going to work that I would contribute positively to the day; behaving otherwise simply wasn't a consideration. I was now living from my Hara and had all the reinforcement I needed for my decision. One particular day that stands out in my memory was when a fellow co-worker with the same attitude as mine asked me how my day was going. I responded, "My day is going great. I've tripped over a few miserable people along the way, but I'm fine." The point being, I don't care how stressful your work place is, or how crabby your coworkers and boss are, especially if they are compelled to take it out on you, because they are the external locus of control people. All they are doing is demonstrating the day they're having and their inability to deal with it; you're not having that kind of a day, so why join them? Have your day.

Whether life provides you with all you desire or protects you from suffering is hardly a measurement of your success or value. Whether you are victorious or defeated, the true value lies in what you do with either result. For example, a few years ago I was watching a newscast where the reporter was interviewing a farmer who'd just had his farm destroyed by a tornado. When the reporter asked him if he ever asked himself, "Why me?" his instantaneous reply was, "I never ask, Why me? I only ask, What can I learn from it?" Do you see my point? Victory shows you what you did right; defeat shows you what you need to do differently next time or the things you can do nothing about. A defeat never means the journey is over, it just means it's a do-over.

Success is an ongoing process punctuated by goal attainment. I have a problem with the thinking some people engage in that ties their self-worth to the outcome of a single event, whether it be one exam, one game, whatever. The object is to repair the flat and keep on driving. You don't give up based on one imperfect result, especially one that can be improved upon. You need to focus on the fix, not the problem. Concentrate you energy on a problem only long enough to identify it. Then quickly move on to solving it. If a house is on fire, what good is it to stand around and say to yourself, "You know what, that house is on fire. Yep, it's on fire. Wow, look at that sucker burn. Man, I sure feel bad about it." You're clearly focusing on the problem not the solution. The victim who gets burned feels bad about the problem and fails to act; the hero focuses on the solution and takes action to resolve the problem. When you want success, blame and fault finding doesn't help, it only preoccupies you and keeps you from moving on. Focus on the fix already, and get back to striving for success.

Embracing and maximizing your control over your two responsibilities will help you fully function in any social situation, whether it is familiar or completely brand new. What are the two aspects of any situation that you have control over? Who you are and what you do. I hear a lot of people say, "But I want to make a good impression." Well, let me ask you, where is a good impression made? In the other person's mind, that's where. Are we mind readers? How are we to know what will make a good impression? If we understand our two responsibilities, then we are unlikely to be overtly disrespectful, or offensive or do anything to cause a bad impression. If we accept responsibility for what we do, how many would choose to cause unpleasantness in someone else's day? Especially when we can no longer make excuses for it, since it is our responsibility, our choice. In trying to impress when you don't know what impression to make, you tend to operate as though you know what will please this other person, and your behaviors become contrived. You create expectations in your mind, and your efforts will help you achieve a goal that is actually out of your reach, thus increasing your anxiety by trying to control what you can't. The likelihood that your efforts will backfire increases when you try to master those factors that are none of your business instead of focusing on the factors that are.

Whenever you set a personal goal that's success is dependent on another person's unpredictable reaction, you're not likely to get it. There's no way of gauging someone else's reaction to you. When you manufacture a lot of good qualities to offer someone, hoping it's what they want, it typically comes across as phoniness. Let me ask you this: How hard is it to spot a salesperson? You can tell when you're being sold something, right? Well, if someone else senses a sales pitch coming from you, it can seem dishonest and make him or her suspicious. This may make them turn off to you, which I'm sure is the opposite of what you want.

But by sticking to your two responsibilities, you put no pressure on yourself to contribute more than you already have. You can offer who you are and what you do to every situation in life, which is all you've got. You will be genuine, confident, relaxed and completely yourself. So put it out there honestly, and confidently, and let any impression to be made take care of itself.

If we accept responsibility for the programming that makes us who we are, that guides what we do in response, then we are fully responsible for the output we contribute to the world. The world we live in today is full of suffering – the kind we create for ourselves and for others as well as the suffering facilitated by the acts of others. By accepting responsibility for our contributions, we can choose either to add to the suffering of the world or relieve some of it. It sounds like a tremendous task, but it's accomplished so simply, with our individual acts, decisions and our acceptance of our true responsibilities. If you're not convinced that just being yourself is sufficient to make a difference in this world, let's consider the benefits for a moment.

When the sun rises it's just being itself, and, as a result, the earth is warmed and life is sustained. The warmth from the sun causes water to evaporate and become a cloud. When the cloud has too much water, it rains and it rains because the cloud is just being a cloud, and, therefore, plants are watered and encouraged to grow. This natural process is so simple and yet so profoundly valuable.

Being human is just like this. When you feel sad, you cry, when you're happy, you laugh. When emotion becomes excessive, you cry, laugh, whatever, to release it. As a cloud rains its excess away, so do you. What remains is simply you. So when inspired to spread kindness, do so. When compelled to share, give. When grateful, love. Just simply who you are. So much additional joy is added to life from these simple acts. All things in life—the sun, the earth, trees, flowers, human beings— exist in their most beautiful state when they are doing nothing more than being themselves. See how powerful a force just being true to your inherent responsibilities can be.

Who we are takes a lot of self-examination to determine. But it is essential to do so, because who we are determines every aspect of our lives. There are plenty of ideas in our heads that serve no other purpose than to make our lives more complicated. They hurt when what we actually need is help. It is up to you to confront those aspects of your programming that are outdated, untrue, harmful and just plain useless. The programming we choose to indulge in means the difference between success in life and failure. We succeed when we are able to accomplish the goals we set for ourselves and, more importantly, when we can contribute positively to the lives of those around us in the process. If you deliberately leave suffering in your wake, you have nothing to teach about success, I don't care what your balance sheet says. If you are not a successful human being first, nothing else you do matters. We experience what we call failure when something inside us sabotages our ability to be successful. Right from the start you need to realize that only successful thinking creates success. If you're not programmed for success, then you obviously won't be successful.

If we program ourselves to expect the worst and are afraid of less than favorable outcomes, we will seldom attempt things. If our programming includes values of growth through new experiences, perseverance and learning from experience, we will be eager to pursue things. Granted, no amount of successful thinking replaces a clear strategy for setting and achieving goals and the means for going about achieving them.

Setting and Working Your Goal

First you made your Hara decision that something has got to change or that you want something more. The question still remains: What do you want? Amazingly this can be a difficult question to answer for some. If you can't answer this question then stop reading right now until you can. You have to know with utmost precision what you are aiming for. Otherwise you might as well be looking for a needle in a haystack, at night, blindfolded, with your hands tied behind your back. When you're driving some place, you can't have a ball park idea where you're going; you need an address, or you'll drive around endlessly until you run out of gas.

Please Visit www.BrianRKing.com

If you do have an answer to the question, "What do I want?" then proceed. But before you do, don't confuse "What do I want" with "What *should* I want?" I've come across too many people who put all of their energy into accomplishing the goals they were raised to think were important (e.g. acquiring cars, money, etc.) and end up characters in a miserable success story. Be sure the question you're asking is "What *do* I want?

I know of many people who complain about the way their lives are and when you ask them what they want to make things better, they don't know. They put so much energy into being dissatisfied that they haven't thought for a second about what it might take to improve things. When you can answer the question, "What do I want?" answer it as specifically as possible. Then you have your goal, and you may proceed.

Thinking Inside Out

After you determine what you want, then do an exercise with yourself that I call "Inside Out." Picture your goal in your head as clearly as a photograph. Describe, in as much detail as possible, how it looks, from every angle. Study it and build it, so that you can see it, feel it and touch it. If you can't see it in great detail, you'll have a hard time recognizing it when you come upon it. Let it become as real to you as your own heartbeat, so that no one can ever convince you that you're experience is unrealistic or impossible.

Then imagine that your goal isn't inside your head anymore; it is actually outside in your life. You have achieved it. Now ask yourself, "How is my life different now that I've achieved this goal? How do I feel about it or about myself?" The greater your commitment to this exercise the more powerful the result. When you do it correctly, you will be left with the experience of achieving your goal and the belief that you have the ability to do so. Like the saying goes, seeing is believing. The only thing that remains is to take the necessary action to make your life look identical to the picture in your head. This exercise is all about setting the stage for making the reality in your head the reality of your life.

Once you've done the Inside Out exercise and know precisely where you're going, you can proceed with determining how you are going to get there. Often, not enough thought is put into a goal to gauge if it will truly create what we want for ourselves—especially if we strive for goals based on the dreams others have for us that we may not truly have for ourselves. In addition, the clearer we can see the treasures that lie in achieving the goal, the greater the incentive for reaching it. To achieve any goal you must proceed step by step: let's begin simply.

The process for accomplishing any goal can be seen as similar to the task of climbing a ladder. There is the starting point, the destination and the steps needed to get there. First you need a goal. Let's use the goal of getting dressed for work in the morning as an example to keep this simple. My starting point is assembling the clothes I intend to put on. What are the steps to get there? The way I do it is:

1. Shirt on

2. Pants on

3. Shoes on

4. Tie on

5. Jacket on

I am dressed for work.

The steps needed to get to the goal of getting dressed are very clear cut. I know what the steps are, and I can tell when they've been completed. If you can't visualize how a goal is going to be accomplished, you can't visualize yourself accomplishing it. Writing down your objectives (i.e. steps required to achieve your goal) helps provide you with a concrete visual of how you need to proceed, just as looking at a ladder lets you know where the next rung is as you're climbing it. Anytime you set a goal, your objectives must be clear, feasible and achievable. If your objectives aren't clear, you won't know when you've accomplished them. If they aren't feasible, meaning you don't have the means to carry them out, then you won't be prepared to achieve them. If your objectives aren't achievable, that is, you aren't capable for whatever reason, then you currently lack the skill to carry them out. Let's say you want to build a house. You've got the blueprints and the objectives clearly spelled out, so you know exactly what you need to do. In this case, your goal and objectives are clear. But you don't have money for the materials, so it isn't feasible. Or let's say you don't have the knowledge of construction required to build a house so it may not be achievable. Your goal can only be reached when the previous challenges are resolved.

By clearly stating what is needed at the outset, you can eliminate as many challenges as possible before you begin. You must know where you want to go, where you are at and what resources you currently have at your disposal. Then you can determine what else is required.

A very important point: You can set a goal for yourself without knowing how you're going to get there. When President Kennedy set the goal to put a man on the moon, he had no idea what it would take to accomplish it. But because his goal was so magnificent, those whose shoulders it fell upon to make it happen did whatever it took to make it real. In my opinion, every goal is feasible and achievable. The point in assessing what your resources are now is so you know what you have to go out and learn or get at the outset so you don't keep tripping over preventable obstacles along the way. If Thomas Edison can take us from candle to lightbulb and the Wright Brothers from ground to flight, then clearly your ability to create anything and everything you want is limited only by your imagination and tenacity.

Partializing

Now that you know how to structure your goal and objectives, there is the matter of how you perceive the process that can determine how overwhelming the task becomes for you. Look back at the list of objectives for getting dressed. Which step do you think is the most important? Many people I've asked have told me they think the last step is the most important because it is the final one, which means they've reached their goal. My answer is different. I think that each step is as important as the others are. The only thing special about the final step or even the goal itself is that it is the last one. It is the standard you established that lets you know when you're done. Face it, there is nothing final about accomplishing a goal. It merely sets the stage for your next project.

Like building a house or getting dressed, each step in the process is of equal importance in reaching the final goal. If the doctors had decided to skip something in my cancer treatment, I don't imagine it would have had the same outcome. If a step is missed or done incorrectly, the quality of the final goal is compromised. If the foundation of the house is not laid with the utmost attention because you're distracted by your eagerness to start putting the walls up, it may not be able to support the walls adequately. If the walls are not strong and sturdy, they will not support the roof. As a result of not partializing (breaking your goal down into smaller steps) and staying focused on the total completion of each objective, the house could come tumbling down.

In reality, the final goal isn't the most important—it's just the last one. As you begin working on your first objective, its completion is your goal, and it demands your undivided attention to be accomplished properly, otherwise you can't begin the next objective. A surgeon can't remove a tumor until the incision is made; there is no room to skip steps.

By writing down your objectives, you have the luxury of only having to think about the current one. The list is there for your reference so you don't need to keep everything in your head that is likely to distract you.

Anyone who wishes to build a house may look at the list of objectives or the immensity of the final goal and say, "Man, that's a daunting task. I don't think I can do it. Why did I ever think I could build a house?" First of all, this is failure thinking, not success thinking. Remember: Only success thinking creates success. When you sit down and partialize your goal, you must embrace only those thoughts that will help you achieve each objective. "I sure hope I don't screw this up" is not an ingredient for success. You don't make a cake with dirt in it, because dirt isn't an ingredient in successfully making a cake. All it will do is make it taste lousy and probably not bake properly, all because you added one useless ingredient. If it doesn't help you, you can't use it, so leave it where you found it. Others might say, "You're a dreamer" or "Keep your feet on the ground" or "Don't set your standards too high—you'll only be disappointed." Or even worse, "You're not smart enough for that" or "You'll never do it." When partializing your goals and picturing the ingredients necessary for achieving them, which of the previous statements will help you to achieve them? That's right none of them. So don't add them to your formula.

The idea of knowingly adding something to a cake that would ruin it seems absurd. But how quickly do we allow the words or actions of others to poison our goals and dreams and negatively affect the outcome. If you can't use it, then lose it. It's that simple.

So what are the thoughts of success? Statements like, "I will do this" or "There is a way and I will find it." Thoughts that keep you solution focused instead of problem/obstacle focused and with success as the only outcome are the keys to victory in the game of life.

Remember, you don't pave roads with mud—you use concrete. Concrete is strong and solid and supports you as you drive toward successful completion of your journey. Using mud for paving has the same effect as using doubt, criticism and unsuccessful thinking when setting or working toward your goal. You sink in it, you can't get good footing, you slip and fall a lot and soon you're covered in it. Now that you're covered in mud, you're so involved in it that you can no longer proceed on your journey. Instead, pave the path toward your goals with concrete as you build and support your objectives with the thoughts of success that will keep you moving forward. Thoughts such as, "This is what is required, and this is how I'm going to do it," are the thoughts of success. Or, "I may not be sure how to do it, but I'm going to find out how." You must visualize the task in your head and its accomplishment, with only success in mind. If you can't see it, you can't achieve it, because it won't appear real and you won't be able to recognize it when you get there.

Early in my high school years, my friends and I would have discussions about what we think we'd be able to deal with if we had to. When we considered if we'd be able to handle having cancer, we all agreed we didn't think we'd be able to. I'm sure this contributed to their reaction to my diagnosis. When it comes down to it, none of us has the slightest inkling what we can withstand until we're called upon to do so. I've heard many stories of elderly grandmothers lifting cars off of grandchildren, an ability they would likely discount in discussion. But when it becomes necessary, guess what happens? One of the greatest human assets is our ability to rise to the occasion. Instead of questioning your ability to do anything, understand that you could if you had to.

Part of dealing with cancer meant I had to learn how to partialize. As I recovered and set my goals for how my life was to become, I had to plan day-to-day what I could do that day based on how weak I was. The most important thing, however, is to do something. There is a simple law of physics that states that things in motion tend to stay in motion, and things at rest tend to stay at rest. So once you begin to pursue a goal, don't stop.

Another thing that can interfere with your ability to stick to the pursuit of your goal, in addition to your own negative thinking, is the criticisms you get from others. Your motivation is for success; ask yourself what their motivation is when they offer destructive vs. constructive criticism. First of all, always remember that everyone is the foremost expert on their own opinion, especially when they mistake it for fact. Some of the biggest lies and misconceptions are delivered with utmost confidence. If someone tries to talk you out of seeking a goal, find out for yourself if his or her reasoning is correct. Even if it is, if you want your goal bad enough, determine what you can do to succeed in light of the new information. Every time Thomas Edison found that a particular filament wouldn't work, he used another. After 10,000 experiments he found the one that worked and successfully invented the lightbulb. He wanted it bad enough, and he refused to give up. Those who may have encouraged him to quit were all wrong. I can't tell you how many times I've heard the phrase, "Trust me, it isn't going to work." If everybody believed that when it was told to them, we'd still be lighting our houses by candle and wondering how the birds do it.

Your own determination may be a threat to others if you're attempting something they were unable or too afraid to do themselves. If you succeed, you rob them of their excuses, which is psychologically dangerous for them. Be wary of how much of their own self-doubt is being flung at you through their comments. If the person you're talking to is someone you tend to compete with, their criticism may be aimed at preventing you from becoming more successful than them. Whatever their motivation, your motivation needs to remain the same: success, success, success, whether it is in career, family, love or life in general. Investing your energy in developing the kind of thinking and skills needed to accomplish the goals you set for yourself is not just an investment in success. It is first and foremost an investment in yourself.

Assembling the Puzzle

Whatever education or skills you acquire as you travel through this life, you are your primary instrument. It is you who utilizes your education and you who practices these skills. In addition to acquiring knowledge, you must actively refine yourself. Make yourself as sharp and effective a tool as you can be. A blunt saw doesn't cut very well. If it does it is a painstaking, exhaustive process because it isn't as sharp as it could be.

We are not only our own primary asset in life; we are also our own primary obstacle. When it comes time to set out to make our way in life, it is our own programming, thoughts, doubts and all that destructive criticism that we tell ourselves that is responsible for holding us back. If an arrow is going to fly straight and hit its target, it must have a smooth shaft, a straight tail and a sharpened point. Otherwise, it could curve in flight and miss the target. That is why it is so important that in shaping and refining ourselves, our make up keeps us flying straight and prevents us from losing track of our target. To refine yourself for success, make sure your destination is always clear, and you are prepared to fly straight, so you can hit your target.

Now let's continue talking about achieving our goals. You know about partializing and thinking for success, but you also need to know how to stay that way. Spending a lot of time looking at the overall goal can cause anxiety because of the size of the task. People don't build houses; houses get built. The goal isn't to build a house; the house is only the endpoint of having achieved the other goals properly. Your first goal may be to cut some lumber (not a daunting task) or to hammer some boards together (not daunting either). Eventually you may have to lay some tile. The point being that completing each step is your goal, so the end result will happen on its own. You simply move to the next objective after the previous one is completed. Of course your eye will glance to the end point because you've set a final goal for yourself. But use you're list of objectives to keep you focused on the immediate task.

Now you know how important your programming and ability to partialize can be. Reprogramming ourselves to think successfully can be difficult and quite challenging. For some, partializing on paper is one thing, but being able to stay that way in your mind is another story. However, as you begin practicing the skill that will be introduced later, you will see how retrainable your programming actually is. But first here's an analogy to help further clarify the value and power of partializing.

Think of every goal you aspire to as a completed puzzle. The steps to achieve it require that the pieces be placed in the correct order. Of course the puzzle may appear vast depending on the size of the goal. Its apparent complexity can be overwhelming. Be that as it may, if you look at the puzzle more closely, what do you see? A series of small, interconnected, unintimidating pieces that comprise the puzzle. You can place each piece in the palm of your hand and observe its modesty. Each solitary piece of the vast puzzle is so minute and simple. It poses no threat to you at all. Now you are no longer focused on the magnitude of the puzzle or the goal. You realize that all that is required of you is to assemble it piece by piece, step by step in order to reach the final goal.

As the puzzle is assembled one piece at a time, life is constructed one moment at a time, and every challenge arises little by little. Life is a unique compilation of pieces that are not all available at the outset. Often you must complete one task before the next one reveals itself. When opportunities present themselves, the challenge then lies in choosing the correct one. The clearer your goal, the easier it should be to see which opportunity will lead you there.

Choosing incorrectly can leave you with a piece that doesn't fit correctly. Such decisions can cause pain in life, as a hole is now left where the correct piece is desperately needed. It is hard to say when the correct piece will present itself again. One lesson to be learned by this is that, although each piece of the puzzle is different, it is complementary to the previous and all others as well. Although small in size, it assists in supporting the entire design. So our decisions and placement are very important, no matter how small a decision it seems to be. This puzzle is never completed in one's lifetime, as our challenges are ongoing. Each moment provides us with an opportunity to improve upon the moment before. Only by being fully aware and focused as the puzzle is constructed can we know which piece will best complement the others. In doing so, the chances are very good that each decision made will be the correct one. The lives we construct will be strong. The regrets in our minds will be none.

CHAPTER FOUR

Taking Life the Only Way It Comes: The Time Cure

Remember that you are only responsible for who you are and what you do in any given moment. I once heard someone say "take life one moment at a time," like this was an option. Of course you have to take life one moment at a time—that's the only way it comes. No matter how hasty our schedule or how limited our patience, life moves at the same rate.

I discovered the profundity of the moment during my stint in isolation during my cancer treatment. I was sitting alone in my room. I noticed the large face of the clock that was hanging on the wall across from me. The room was absolutely silent, and the ticking of the clock was deafening. As I followed the rhythm of the clock, I noticed that it seemed to synchronize with the beating of my own heart. Counting the moments of my life. It was from this that I came to realize that life occurs in moments. It didn't happen in minutes, hours or days. I understood that each heartbeat was the beginning and end of each opportunity in my life. The more I focused on my heartbeat, the rhythm of the clock and each and every moment, the more I realized a greater sense of peace. I was now less inclined to anticipate and become anxious about a future that didn't exist until I made it or to obsess about the pains from my past. This experience was the beginning of moment-to-moment living for me. Now I will teach you how to begin to do the same.

Moment to Moment

This next step will show you how to begin moment-to-moment living. Find a clock with a second hand on it. Watch the second hand for a minute or so. Tick, tick, tick. It progresses smoothly, no haste, no impatience. It proceeds in a constant rhythm. Now consider some of the expressions we use to describe time: "time seems to be dragging along," "time flies," "running out of time," "wasted time." Time doesn't drag or fly, it's steady. Nor can we waste it or run out of it; it has an eternal supply. What changes is our awareness, and that's something that can be wasted. So let's see if we can start to view time differently, more closely to how it actually is.

The Moment Hand

From this moment on, every time you see a clock do not view this moving arm as a second hand. Instead, refer to it as a moment hand. Although the clock face is typically segmented as though to imply that time is broken up in some way, you can see that the second hand is not inhibited, its progress not impeded. Our perception of time, however, has always been an impediment to us and a source of great stress. There seems to never be enough of it, or it goes too quickly.

In actuality, time is a manmade concept; it isn't what we perceive it to be. Neither time, nor life, occurs in seconds, hours or days. Life occurs in moments—one moment at a time, strung together like pearls on a necklace. Hence the designation of the moment hand on the clock. I find this to be a more accurate designation of the actual quality of time.

The clock is a tangible representation of the actual moment-to-moment speed of life.

With this new perception of time as an unlimited commodity, there is always enough, so much so that it loses its constrictive quality. It's not in a rush, so why should we be? Even in man's attempt to design an instrument to master the length of his day, he was uncontrollably bound by the moment-to-moment movement of life. Clocks surround us all day long. When we apply pressure to ourselves to compel us to move faster than the speed of life, we will inevitably burn ourselves out with stress. You can't move faster than life. It's the equivalent of reaching for something that's out of your reach and stretching so far that you pull a muscle. All because you tried to reach for something clearly out of your grasp. The discomfort of stress is like a pulled muscle that results from trying to move faster than the speed of life—from trying to carry a burden or responsibility that is beyond us to carry.

Moving at the Speed of Life

From now on a clock need not only be a measure of this thing we call time. It can also serve as a reminder to reorient and calm yourself. You can begin by taking a minute to watch the moment hand and return your awareness to the moment-to-moment speed of life—the actual pace at which things are accomplished rather than the anxiety-building speed we are encouraged to live at. This way a clock is transformed from an object that compels us to hurry to a reminder to calm and pace ourselves. You might as well embrace the fact that life must be worked with one moment at a time, because that's the only way it comes. As you might recall, earlier in this book I discussed watching a tree outside my hospital window. I discussed how it taught me to adjust to adversity, gradually, as it arose moment to moment. Let me now expand on that idea.

While watching the tree I noticed that before the wind blew, the tree was calm, perfectly still. It didn't seem to be in anticipation of anything. Whenever a breeze or a gust appeared, it simply adjusted. It didn't resist the wind nor did it topple over in submission. It just patiently and flexibly adjusted until the adversity of the wind subsided. Then once again, it became calm and still.

I realized that the tree seemed to understand that the adversity of the wind was temporary and that the wind would soon be gone. It didn't overreact to a gentle breeze that caused an excessive bend in the branches. It just dealt with what it was given. I realized at that point in my illness that I had been seeing adversity as just adversity and reacted the same way at every turn—strongly. I also responded based on my memories of past adversity. The tree didn't appear to do that.

The tree helped me realize that my adversities actually happen in degrees. As the tree endures a never-ending change from gentle breeze to gust to calm, it will simply adjust. In the tree's case, adversity is not positive or negative, only an opportunity for its branches to stretch.

The tree lives in the present with what is actually here; it doesn't wait bent in anticipation of a future wind or stay bent after a past wind subsides. It sits in peace without a sound, and if the wind should blow again, it adjusts accordingly then allows the wind to go.

I realized that I could begin to practice these qualities. When the winds of my adversity subsided, I would allow myself to become still. I would concern myself only with present tasks before me. I'm sure there were many opportunities to find calmness throughout my ordeal, but because I was wrapped up in resenting what had happened and fearing what was to come, I missed those opportunities.

As the tree does, I would no longer concern myself with a wind that wasn't here. When one arises, I decided I would embrace the same spontaneity as I adjust. It started to appear useless to focus on the inconvenience of the adversity I faced, or obsess over how much I'd like it to be different. Wishing for life to be different wouldn't change the fact that I had to deal with what was before me before anything could change.

So from that moment on, my goal was to adjust as required to any degree of breeze or gust—no more overreactions. As the breeze subsided, I would relax and be calm. The resilience of the tree doesn't belong to it. It is only a mechanism that is inherent in nature that the tree actively utilizes. We all embody the patient resilience practiced by the tree. But we need to learn to practice it.

Minding the Breath, Minding the Hara

Moment-to-moment living cannot be embraced if you only understand it conceptually. You have to feel it if you're going to practice it. The best way I've found to experience the moment is in the experience I first had in the hospital when I experienced the breath moving in and out of my body, moment to moment. As I refined this practice, I found it to be a powerful way to center my mind and tap into the power of my Hara. Through this exercise I learned to embrace change (inhalation/exhalation) and increase my ability to remain mentally alert, focused and calm. This is essential to functioning fully in any circumstance. So here's how to practice "minding the breath."

First I would suggest finding a comfortable place to sit down. A comfortable chair will do, one where your feet lie flat on the ground and the back of your thighs rest flat on the chair. You're looking for a spot where you can sit comfortably and sit straight without the need to constantly readjust yourself. You must sit so that you can sit up straight. Your hands should be resting comfortably on your lap but close to your abdomen. If they are too far out your shoulders will round forward and you will no longer be sitting up straight.

Now, point your face straight ahead but cast your eyes gently down about two-thirds of the way. Your eyes should be open, but they shouldn't be focusing on anything. You should be concerned only with feeling your breath, not looking at anything. You may want to face a blank wall so your eyes won't be inclined to wander around. Next, relax your shoulders and then the rest of your body. You only want enough tension to maintain your posture. You must be relaxed to practice calmness but not so relaxed that you feel drowsy. You're training your mind for alertness and focus, not sloth.

Once your posture is stable, just begin to feel your breathing. Breathe in and out through your nose, and allow your breaths to naturally become deep. This is not lung breathing we're talking about; you should be feeling your abdomen rise and fall. You are breathing from your Hara for this exercise. Allow your Hara to become filled with air. It is important here to see the connection between your Hara being essential to life as it is the pool of your breath.

You may be tempted to force yourself to breathe deeper but don't. You're body naturally breathes more deeply when it is calm. So just allow the breathing to happen on its own, and you will gradually feel it deepen. Relax your abdomen as you breathe so that your diaphragm can easily expand and your lungs can fill completely. The more relaxed the abdomen, the deeper the breath.

Lastly, the manner in which you mind or mentally watch your breath is essential. As I said before, your breathing is happening spontaneously, and you are not manipulating it in any way. You simply watch your breathing as though it were a sunset with an instant replay. The abdomen rises, and the abdomen falls. The breath moves in, the breath moves out. Watch each inhalation, and each exhalation. Observe moment to moment.

This is the most important point for this exercise, so pay attention. If it is your desire to learn to live from your Hara, then you must master minding the breath as it falls into your Hara. As you are minding your breath, you are minding your center. Therefore, your mind becomes centered. There is nothing clearer and more focused than a centered mind, so practice this diligently. With enough practice, minding your breath will be all that is required to center your mind and work from your Hara.

As you practice minding the breath, you may begin to experience thoughts running through your mind, such as everything you have to do today. This is common because when your mind is clear, anything can fly in to try and take your mind away. So you need to practice taking your mind back. When you notice that you've become distracted, all you need to do is acknowledge that fact and return to minding your breath. Eventually, with much practice, the thoughts that enter won't even catch your attention; they will just enter and leave.

In doing this you are practicing keeping your mind focused on exactly what you're doing at this moment, which is watching your breath. When a thought of something else rushes in, you're simply putting it aside and getting back to what you're doing. Eventually, this ability will work its way into every activity in your life so that you'll be able to focus intensely with little or no distraction.

You should practice this exercise for no less than five minutes at a time, as it may take a bit for your mind and breath to become calm. Half an hour or more at a time is ideal. Don't be upset with yourself if you aren't able to perfect this technique right away. Your mind can be like a racehorse that was just let out of the gate. It may take time for it to slow down. Be diligent and patient. Your mind will become more and more trainable, but you must practice and practice often.

As I said, through this practice you learn not to become distracted by things that are not related to what you're doing. You learn to stay on task by concentrating precisely on what's happening in this moment. No matter how busy the environment is around you, you are concerned with where you're at in that situation and tending to it. This is a powerful tool. Once your mind is trained for this, you can walk into chaos and remain calm. After all, this practice teaches you not to control or manipulate your breath or the thoughts racing through your mind but just watch them and let them be. You look to control yourself instead. Walking through a chaotic office or school day is no different. Control yourself, watch the situation, understand it and then act according to your two responsibilities.

Let's continue exploring just how relevant this practice is in everyday life. We often speak in terms of the past or the future as if these were tangible entities. In actuality, the past is gone—done, finished. The past is done with us whether or not we are done with the past. All we have to work with now are the present consequences and present opportunities. After experiencing unforeseen consequences I often hear people say, "I should've done this, or I could've done that." In essence, putting their mental energy on a desire to make a repair of the past that can't be made. This gets you nowhere. Instead, work with what you have, not with what is gone. The results are your building blocks.

The other side of this coin is the future, which is fantasy. The future is nothing but a projection; a story we construct based upon our own ideals about what we wish things to be for us next. You can't do anything there either. I'm not saying it's bad to set goals for ourselves or to think about those goals. Goals are essential. But where is the work done to achieve these goals? Right here, right now, in the present.

When running a marathon, the consideration of running 26 miles can be overwhelming and even discouraging. The end point is not the only point but one of many. Your task lies in tending to each step, or each moment, of the process literally. As your awareness lies with each step, your task becomes the process as opposed to a far-off destination. Just as the ocean begins with a single drop of water, any seemingly over-whelming task can become as simple and manageable. Sitting and watching your breath for half an hour or more may seem difficult, but your actual task is watching a single breath. If you keep doing that, before you know it half an hour has passed.

Minding the breath can be difficult to master, but it is one of the best ways for mastering the Hara mindset. If you wish to begin more simply,

I will teach you another method for mastering the moment in the next chapter of this book.

Calming your mind can be difficult, but so is calming the body and minimizing the stress it carries. The key to beginning to relieve stress and tension in your life is to first know that you are experiencing them. I am a practitioner of the Japanese healing art called Shiatsu, which utilizes pressure points on the body to help resolve many ailments, including tension brought on by stress. Often as I work on someone who claims to be relaxed, I find several points on his or her body that are solid balls of tension. These points feel like tight knots, and when I press on them the person yells in pain. In spite of how obviously tense these people are, they either lack the self-awareness to realize it or they are tense and stressed as a matter of routine and have just become psychologically desensitized to it's presence in their lives and bodies.

But as any physician will tell you, whether you are aware of the stress you have in your life or not, enduring it long term without buffering it in some way can have damaging consequences, like ulcers, heart disease or a weakening of the immune system to name a few. Minding the breathing as you've just learned is wonderful for calming the mind, which of course will gradually calm the body. But there are other exercises that can calm the body more quickly and deeply. These techniques will increase your awareness of your body as readily as minding the breathing increases your awareness of your mind. It stands to reason that the more aware you are of your body, the more quickly you will notice tension beginning to build so you can begin preventing it from doing so. As you first learn these exercises, they may seem incredibly detailed and lengthy. But once you're familiar with them and become proficient, they may take no more than a few minutes to complete.

External Body Scan

The first technique is called the External Body Scan. The second is the Internal Body Scan, which is a bit more difficult but very important as our insides suffer greater damage from stress than our outsides. We will start with the External Body Scan.

This technique is to aid you in becoming aware of every inch of your body, especially in assisting you in determining the spots on your body where you store stress. You begin by finding a quiet place to lie down. It needs to be quiet so you can concentrate, and you need to be able to lie flat on your back with your arms at your side. Once you are lying down, close your eyes and relax as much as possible before beginning. Start minding your breath so that your breathing becomes deep. Once you have been breathing deep for a minute or two, begin to scan your body.

Direct your attention to the top of your head. Focus on it as though the rest of your body doesn't exist. Concentrate on relaxing the top of your head and letting the tension dissolve, releasing the muscles. You can also use your exhalation so that you relax that part of your body as you breath out. It's like you're exhaling your tension. Sometimes it's helpful to flex the muscles in question and then release them completely, but I find it more useful to just relax the muscles from the point they are at.

Next move your attention to your forehead; when it is relaxed, move to your nose, then your cheeks, your ears and then your jaw. It's perfectly fine if your mouth falls open from relaxing your jaw—don't feel you have to close it. Now relax the back of your head, and this will complete the relaxation of the muscles in your head and face. Before moving on, gradually move your attention through all of the areas of your head and face one more time to make sure none of them have tensed up again. If they have, simply repeat the process as before to release them. When you're head and face are completely relaxed you can move on.

The second part of your body you focus on is your neck. Begin with the back of the neck, and slowly feel the tension releasing from the left side followed by the right. As you move below the head, you will relax things from one side to the other, so choose which side you are going to relax first and stay will that side consistently. Now continue relaxing your neck. Relax the sides of the neck and then the front.

From the front of your neck, slowly draw your attention out along one of your shoulders and relax the area between your neck and shoulder one side at a time. Then relax each shoulder. After your shoulders are completely relaxed, begin moving your attention down your upper arm. Relax the back of your upper arm and then the front. Next relax your elbow. Now begin relaxing your lower arm. Then relax your wrist followed by the back of your hand and the palm of your hand. Finally, relax each finger one at a time. Scan this arm one more time to make sure none of the muscles have tensed again, then complete the same process with the other arm. When both arms are relaxed, move to your upper chest.

Bring your attention back to the front of your neck, and slowly relax the pectoral/breast area of your upper chest. Focus on each muscle of the front of your chest individually and thoroughly. Then relax each side of your chest (the area that would be covered if you put your arms against your sides). Next draw your attention to your abdomen, and relax the entire thing as deeply as you can. Now scan your chest and abdomen again before moving on.

Move your attention to the back of your neck, and then focus on the area between your shoulder blades. Then relax one shoulder blade at a time. Now move your attention slowly down your spine, and relax it as you go (only your spine, not the back muscles). Once this is done, return your focus to one of your shoulder blades, then gradually move your attention down that side of your back, relaxing the muscles as you go. Once reaching the top of the buttock on that side, start over with the other side. After finishing the back the first time, relax it again, but this time relax both sides simultaneously. Some people find it difficult to get the back to relax one side at a time, so this can be a helpful way to finish this part of the body.

Next you want to relax your buttocks, then one leg at a time. Slowly relax the back of your upper leg, then the front, then relax your knee. When finished with that, you want to relax your lower leg, front and back, and the bottom of the foot followed by the top. Like the fingers, relax each toe one at a time. Then do the same with the other leg. If you like, you can quickly scan your body from head to toe once more to smooth everything out.

Now that you've scanned the outside of your body, you've probably discovered those parts of your body that seemed unusually tense. Whether it is the area between the neck and shoulders, between your shoulder blades, or the lower back or the abdomen. Using this exercise to tune into each part of your body is intended to make you more aware of how your body feels in a relaxed state. This way when tension begins to build you are quickly aware of it and can mentally isolate that area and begin to relax it. This is what the external body scan is for. In the long run, you'll no longer have those days where you come home with a stiff neck from having saved that tension until the end of the day; instead you'll be working with it the whole time.

I wouldn't recommend working on the internal body scan until you're familiar with the external one. It helps to have well-developed concentration, relaxation and visualization skills before moving on.

Internal Body Scan

The internal body scan is designed to help you to release the internal tension of your body. Think of your body's tension as a volcano. Deep below the surface you have the pressure building, and eventually it surfaces in knots in your neck muscles or lower back pain. So, to calm the volcano, you need to go deeper. We started with the external body scan because those feelings of tension are more evident and it's easier to train your awareness.

The external body scan focuses primarily on relaxation, but the point of this exercise is more along the lines of imagery. You have to mentally release the tension inside you. Some of it is easy to locate. All you need to do is find a place on your body that feels uncomfortable or painful. Although it may be due to an injury, chances are your own dislike of the presence of pain is intensifying your experience of it. Or maybe you have a pain you just can't explain. Either way, in order to relieve that pain, you need to go through a simple process.

Find a quiet place, and assume a comfortable position. Bring your awareness into that area of your body that's causing you discomfort; you may even want to place your hand over the area if it helps you to focus. Next, to ask yourself, "If this pain or discomfort could speak, what would it say?" Begin to speak out loud on your pain's behalf; you may be surprised by what it has to say. I have often found my lower back pain to be in response to nervousness. So I do this exercise and verbalize my nervousness, and I talk for as long as it takes. But remember, in order to relieve the nervousness or whatever feeling you're currently experiencing, you have to replace it with reassurance. Statements like, "It can be scary to do _____, but I know I have it in me to do it, and I'm going to do well no matter what the outcome." In this way you're not denying your frustration, you acknowledge it, but you're also acknowledging your own competence. It's kind of like giving yourself a mental hug. There are still deeper tensions we may not be as aware of, however. Here's how we get at them.

It is probably a good idea to complete the external body scan before beginning the internal scan. This way your mind is primed for deliberately bringing about relaxation in the body, and the ability to feel and picture relaxation taking place is readily available. Since you've just completed the external body scan, you should already be on your back and well relaxed. To assist you in concentrating on each organ as you tend to it, you're going to use one of your hands.

Remember that you're not supposed to feel your organ relaxing; this exercise is designed more for you to just be compassionate toward yourself and become more aware of those parts of your body where stress and tension can cause harm. This exercise is a way for you to cultivate peace in your body. Allow your breathing to become deep as you proceed.

Start with the organ whose location is not difficult to find. Take your hand, and place it on the center of your upper chest over your heart. In the previous exercise your mind focused on the surface of the body; now your mind needs to focus deeper. Begin by focusing your mind on the skin beneath the surface of your hand. Then slowly allow your mind to sink into your body about three inches until you can picture yourself inside the organ in question. In this case, feel yourself inside your beating heart, and picture it pumping life-giving blood throughout your body. Feel it contract, imagine its strength.

If emotions are weighing heavily on your heart, then allow them to beat to the surface, because this is the heart's time to be cared for. Feel the emotion reach through the skin on your chest and through your hand where it disperses in the air. This may not make the emotions or the feelings go away completely, but it should at least help you tap into them.

Now slide your hand straight down slowly until your thumb rests just below the bottom of the sternum, which is the bone your hand was just sliding down. At this point your hand is resting on a portion of your liver. Your liver is responsible for cleaning the refuse and many of the poisons from your body. Again, begin with your attention on the skin beneath your hand. Then allow your mind to sink into your liver. Picture your liver, and be grateful for its protection of the rest of your body. Imagine how it is filtering the poison from your blood and how important it is for you to minimize its workload through your own habits. Place your mind inside your liver, and mentally push your image of the toxins in your blood through your liver and then out.

Move your hand to the left until it is on your lower ribcage. Your hand is now resting on part of your stomach. This is one of the few internal organs you can feel working, especially when it is upset. As your hand rests upon it and your mind sinks into it, imagine it calming down. Picture it relaxing as you would a muscle. Spend a little time concentrating on it and encouraging it to function well. Rest your mind inside it as you would rest it if you were laying your heed on a pillow. Picture your stomach as soft, without tension.

Now place your hand over your belly button. You're now in the general location of your intestines, which can become quite upset and loose when you're under stress. As your hand rests over your abdomen, imagine your intestines moving strongly and smoothly. Move your mind into them. Feel how they are strong but relaxed. They are healthy and keeping themselves cleansed. Rubbing your abdomen in a clockwise fashion as you are picturing your intestines can help this image. Allow your mind to follow beneath your hand as it moves in a circle across your belly, and mentally work to push the toxins through and out.

Lastly, return your hand to the position over your navel. This time focus on your abdomen as it rises and falls. Sink your attention into your Hara. Through this motion you will focus on your lungs. Feel your abdomen rise as your breath becomes deeper. Feel your abdomen fall as your lungs release the old stale air from your body. Allow your awareness to be filled with each inhalation and exhalation as your lungs fill your body with the life-giving oxygen that you need. Feel how clear and strong your lungs are. Feel how much more alive you become with each breath.

You may also spend some time minding your breath at the end of this exercise. This is a great opportunity to strengthen your Hara and your awareness of it since you are so relaxed and better able to concentrate.

Spend as much time on each organ as is necessary for your image of its proper functioning to become clear. This is not to say that your imagery will improve its functioning, but it should improve you awareness of its function and thus your treatment of yourself.

Now lay your hand back at your side and relax for a few minutes. Clearly we did not cover every organ of the body, but we did cover the major ones. Again, the idea here is increased awareness of where stress can be stored in the body. The more you see it coming and building, the better you will be at heading it off.

Minding the breath and the external and internal body scans are profound methods for training your mind to live moment to moment and for experiencing how your body and mind are being effected in each moment. After all, the moment is where life occurs and where you have the greatest opportunity to be most effective in life. In the next chapter you will learn a skill that will allow you to put all of this training into action. Now that you can live in the moment while relaxing, let's learn how to do it on the move.

CHAPTER FIVE

Immediacy

As I promised, I will now teach you a less complicated way of mastering the moment until you become comfortable with the minding the breath exercise. The "Immediacy Skill," although easier to grasp, is made more powerful when backed with the abilities cultivated while minding the breath. So this is not an either or kind of thing; you must practice and utilize both.

One added benefit of this new technique is that you are not sedentary, or in a resting state, while you practice it. You are actively going about your everyday life. Keep in mind that this skill helps your mind touch only the surface of moment-to-moment living because it employs your thoughts to master the moment. Hopefully you discovered that the minding the breath exercise allows you to get a richer, fuller experience of the moment.

As with minding the breath, the immediacy skill enables you to focus on precisely what you're doing now. This allows you to be more productive and efficient because you are difficult to distract. I have found that the fewer distractions people indulge in, internal or external, the clearer their perceptions are of exactly what needs to be done, both in the short term and long term. In order to be effective long term, you must be effective short term, which means you must be effective every single moment. Toward that end you must master immediacy, which is what this skill is all about.

The immediacy skill leads to increased focus and reduction of stress even in the most adverse situations. As I mentioned, this skill is actually part of the process of the activity you're engaged in. What you're doing actually helps you to relax and focus. Those who have had the opportunity to learn and utilize this skill have expressed a significant reduction in the stress of their everyday lives. They describe how they experience an increased ability to focus, which results in greater productivity both at work and in their private lives. There is no reason why you shouldn't reap the same benefits. Now it is time for you to begin learning and applying the immediacy skill.

The Immediacy Skill

As you embrace the responsibility for who you are and what you do, you need to begin to hone in on operating in the present. At any given time of the day, as you are pursuing any goal, you may find yourself getting carried away with thoughts about your task. This brings us to:

Rule #1: Don't lose track of your head.

In other words, keep your head and your body in the same place—in the present. Don't let your mind spend too much time in the future because your body is always in the present. Likewise, don't let your mind dwell in the past while your body is in the present. This is how we experientially tear ourselves in half. Our mind is drudging up a previous experience while the body is having the current one.

We can become "headless" when we begin to spin stories in our head about all of the things that might happen if the responsibility isn't carried out or if the goal isn't achieved. We begin "what-ifing" every decision we make. What if I make the same mistake as last time? What if it isn't as good as last time? What if I fail? What if others don't like it? How many of the "What-ifs" involve the potential of uncontrollable factors getting in our way? What-ifing and supposing are the fertilizers for anxiety. What-ifing to the point of inaction is a cancerous process that steals energy you could otherwise use to take action. What-ifs have nothing to do with the "what is" of your task. Your thoughts need to focus on what you can do to achieve success, not on the hypothetical threats to it that you can't control. What you're doing is the reality, not your internal chatter about fearing loss of control in aspects of life where you can never have it. It's time to realize that the uncontrollables take care of themselves, whether we fret about them or not. The sun comes up whether we worry about it or not. Whether we wake up at all each day sets the stage for our next move. Our only controllables are our two responsibilities—everything else is out of our hands. We only need give them the necessary acknowledgment when they arise. In that we take them into consideration as pieces of the puzzle, but we don't invest ourselves in them.

As our mind can be prone to preoccupy itself with the uncontrollables, it is our responsibility to bring it back to what it is actually doing, since that's its only responsibility. Now that we know we can only have full control over who we are and what we do and that the place we can maximize them is in the present, now is the time to learn how this is done: by using the Immediacy Skill. Start simple.

Every morning you wake up and go through your own ritual that prepares you for the day. When I was sick this was simple because what was simple was all I could rely upon. Since I felt I couldn't plan for much else I simply concentrated on what I was doing, and this became a profoundly valuable awareness skill.

So as you prepare for your day, at any given point you may notice your mind begin to spin in great detail about every little thing that must be accomplished that day. I have to go here and do this, then after that, and on and on. But soon you realize that this spinning has nothing to do with what you're doing at the time. So bring your mind back to the present by telling yourself what you're actually doing. If you're combing your hair when your mind starts spinning, tell yourself silently, "I'm combing my hair." Keep telling yourself that until that's all your mind is doing. If you're eating your breakfast, say to yourself, "I'm eating breakfast." Or even more immediate "I'm lifting the spoon." After a while you can focus simply on the action: combing, eating, lifting, gradually training your body and mind to concentrate on the immediate task with your undivided attention. This is how you keep your head and body in the present together. In doing so you have just accomplished immediacy or mindfulness, which is the deliberate, conscious involvement in the present. Before long you won't have to think about doing this—it will become automatic. You will become naturally focused.

Granted, the spinnings in your head may revolve around important tasks, but they are irrelevant until the conditions arise under which they can be accomplished. Having to complete a task at work is hardly doable while your current task is brushing your teeth. When you get to work, whatever you're doing then is your task; everything at home is finished and gone so now you can concentrate on work. "I'm signing this document" or "I'm dialing the phone." You'll be presently surprised at how effective this is. You learn not how to put in an eight-hour day but concentrated moments of time. Which do you think is easier and less stressful to do?

Rule #2: Get off the time machine.

This rule is similar to Rule #1 and is offered more as an easier way to conceptualize this mental activity now that you've received some explanation. In other words, stop running to the future that isn't here yet. Stop shoulding a past that can't be revisited or fixed. This mental Ping-Pong game will keep you tripping over the present but seldom stopping there.

Another thing you can do to get off the time machine is to ask your-self a question whenever you start to feel anxious. Anxiety is more or less rooted in anticipation of past discomforts returning or an uncer-tain future approaching. When this occurs, ask yourself, where am I? Then make the answer as immediate as possible (e.g. I'm lying in bed, I'm sitting in a chair, I'm standing, I'm breathing), all of which are stress-free activities and not anxiety-producing. Even if you're at work, (e.g. I'm sitting at my desk or, the less stressful, I'm just sitting), embrace the immediacy until your thinking is consumed with the pres-ent and the anxiety falls away. Once you have reestablished yourself in the present, in a calm activity, then a calm, focused, present-minded state is the place from where you proceed when you begin your next activity. It can be this way all the time as long as you practice this skill. The more immediate and the more focused you are, the less distractible you are to the temptations of the time machine.

This skill is especially useful when you're trying to fall asleep but can't keep your mind from racing. Keep telling yourself, "I'm lying down," "I'm resting" or whatever you say to yourself. It has the same effect as counting sheep. You can even practice minding your breath. By keeping your mind occupied, you no longer focus on the thoughts caus-ing your mind to race. The phrase you repeat to yourself does not pro-duce stress, so you can't help but relax more and more until you're asleep. After a while you will likely find that when you lie down for the night, your brain will just stop spinning and you will fall asleep quicker because you've trained it to do that. Neat, huh?

This is only one of many small ways you can learn to take control back. Your sense of personal control increases when you take control where you have it. Your sense of a loss of control comes from stressing over things you wouldn't have control over whether you stressed about them or not. So take them out of the equation. Keep your energy where it can be of use. You will see your stress decrease, and your confidence and sense of self-efficacy increase.

After a while bringing yourself back to what you're actually doing will teach you to automatically assess what you can and can't do in any given moment. This is because you're paying attention to the needs of the present task instead of chasing expectations and uncontrollables. Once that is assessed, any factors beyond that are not brought into consideration, and there is no room for useless stress over the situation. You will learn to determine what you can do and concentrate your energy on doing it, with complete focus and confidence.

Now as you begin to utilize these concepts and practice the immediacy skill, you will find the serenity from no longer chasing after the things you cannot change. You will find a greater sense of security and control in your life as you embrace the two responsibilities over which you have complete control. The more you practice, the greater your wisdom will become in determining where you are responsible and in control and where you are not. You will be able to cure the cancerous thinking brought on by your misconceptions about time.

Be Like Water

I want to end this chapter with one more image to sear the values of flexibility, spontaneity and the ability to maximize who you are and what you do. I believe that in life, the greatest example of the power of these values lies in the example set by the most abundant substance on this planet: water. We human beings are at least 65% water. It is time we started acting like it.

If you watch the behavior of water, you will better understand how to be like water. When poured into a glass, water becomes the glass. When poured into a pitcher, water becomes the pitcher. It is formless and shapeless, adjusting easily to any situation. It can be liquid, ice or steam, whatever is required of it in response to environmental demands. It traverses all obstacles or wears them down with patience and perseverance. It bathes, nourishes, and supports all of life, all the while adjusting to the requirements of each moment, without losing its essential character. Be like water, and you'll be successful in handling every situation. All of the potential you possess comes from within you. So much of you already is made of water, so use what you've got. Do all you can, that's all you can do. Give all you can, that's all you can give. Give everything you have, because you have everything to give. Be like water.

CHAPTER SIX

Living the Cure

Your Hara decision has been made. You have been minding your breath and tapping into the boundless energy, focus and confidence that comes from doing everything from a state of balance and a strong center. Now it is time to bump it up a notch. Your cauldron of conviction and determination is gurgling—now it's time to make it boil.

If you truly want to be successful in life and have cancer-free thinking, then you must proceed without excuses. Success begins when excuses end. Excuses are the same as placing blame; whatever didn't work need only be viewed from the standpoint of improvement. If you fall short of your goal, your first question isn't "Who's fault is it?" or "What did I do wrong?" Ask only, "How can it be done differently?" No matter how many times circumstances frustrate you, you must be careful not to fall into the blackhole of victimhood. This is the self-absorbed pity party we throw for ourselves when times are tough. I fell into it when I was sick, and I realized the toll it took.

The Blackhole of Victimhood

What I refer to as the blackhole of victimhood is the mental process we go through when something happens to us that makes us sad or feel sorry for ourselves. We begin to focus on our bad feelings, and thus our thoughts become negative as well. "I feel so sad. I'm so depressed.

Nobody likes me." This kind of negative self-indulgence can, and often does, become all-consuming.

A blackhole to the best of my knowledge is created by an object whose gravitational pull is so incredible that is sucks everything into itself—not even light can escape it. The role of the victim accomplishes the same goal: It effectively devours the light of hope and leaves only darkness. Victim thinking is one of the biggest cognitive cancers there is. It dominates your entire life with powerlessness and hopelessness. When you are in an unfavorable situation, and you focus on what you don't like about it at the exclusion of any other thoughts, this mindset begins to consume you and swallow you up. Then you begin to attract greater negativity toward yourself because this is what your mind is focused on. If you think negative, then negative is all you will ever see.

If you are unsatisfied with any part of your life, there is one solution: Get off your butt and change it. If you plant a garden in which the seeds are present to grow the sweetest vegetables the world has ever known, and then you spend all of your time watering and fertilizing the weeds, then what will grow? The victim mentality accentuates the negative. The more you water the weeds, the more choked off the vegetables get.

No matter how severe our circumstances are or how traumatic an event may have been to us, the effect of the actual event never compares to how much we victimize ourselves afterward. As we punish ourselves based on hindsight or continue to pour cognitive gasoline on our fears, our perception or fixation on the assault to our sense of security can magnify our victimization incessantly. That's why control must be taken back immediately. You must separate yourself from those factors that have nothing to do with you so that you don't spend so much time on them that you begin to take mental ownership of them and get caught in the blackhole.

Your energy must be on growth not stagnation. Focus on gain not loss. I have spoken to many people who seem to be wallowing in their own misery like a pig in the mud. They are covered in it and can't see it.

One of them even argued with me and said, "Sometimes you just have to let people feel bad." I thought this was some of the worst advice I'd ever heard. To me this is like standing in a burning house and making no effort to leave it because you feel entitled to burn. Before long the house will be destroyed and you along with it. If you are caught up in a destructive process, you have to get out. One might argue that people will come around in their own time. I don't agree with the rock-bottom philosophy of intervention any more than I think you should allow a house to burn down to its foundation before you try and rescue the people inside. Wallowing in your own self-pity is like riding an exercise bike: It uses up a lot of energy and gives you something to occupy your time, but it doesn't get you anywhere.

You need to begin to get out of the victim role the moment you find yourself in it. A person's own time varies when it comes to completing the journey, but at least get them on the path. The victor in you is the only thing that can save the victim in you. Remember that your circumstances are never bigger than you are. As I said before, if you want to change something, you must replace it. So here is a cure for victim thinking.

A Cure for Victim Thinking

The most important thing to realize is that we are often victimized more by the words and thoughts we use to describe an event than the actual event. To start with, we need to exchange verbs. We typically use words to describe our feelings like "scared," "frightened," "depressed," "trapped," "overwhelmed," "confused," "frustrated," etc. If you notice the common attribute of these words is that they all end in "ed." Using words like the ones above that end in "ed" is often referred to as "hidden victim language (Canfield, 2000)." It creates the impression in our minds that something was done to us; something scared us, overwhelmed us or made us feel trapped. When what really happened was that we did these thing to ourselves. To fully understand this, let's rewrite the "ed" words so that they end in "ing."

Remember the idea here is to take back responsibility for yourself. So instead of being "scared" by something else, you're actually "scaring" yourself as well as "frightening," "depressing," "trapping," "overwhelming," "confusing," and "frustrating" yourself. These feelings are the results of the thoughts you use to describe an experience to yourself. Some people expend a lot of energy depressing themselves by focusing on what they think is wrong and punishing themselves for it. Get the idea? When you realize that these experiences are your own creation, you can choose not to create them or at the very least to create them differently. Use the same techniques you learned with the internal body scan and the immediacy skill: Realize that you're scaring or depressing yourself, and show compassion for yourself, then recognize where you actually are and what you're actually doing. This will help you to separate the event from the response until you eventually train yourself to create a powerful response instead of a victimizing response. By recognizing the power you have, you begin to stand as a victor in all circumstances and retire the victim.

Now You Know

Throughout this book you've received some pretty powerful tools to allow you to become more successful in life by ridding yourself of the cancerous cognitive tumors that steal your productive energies. But success isn't just a series of accomplishments or positive thoughts. It is an attitude, a mindset that informs your actions. Successful people are made not born. If a computer isn't programmed to accomplish the tasks you want it to, it simply won't. The same goes for you. If you want to be successful you have to be programmed for it. For starters, you know the two responsibilities that will truly allow you to make a difference in your own life and the lives of others, solely because you have complete control in how they're carried out. You can now begin to use time as a sail instead of a straightjacket. It frees you by reminding you to relax and pace yourself. Time is a continuum and finding where we landed on it makes as much sense as spending billions of dollars trying to find the corners of the universe. Realizing where you aren't doesn't help you accomplish anything where you are. The Immediacy Skill taught you that the only place you can do your best is in the task before you. If you're going to build a house, your mind has to be on the brick you're about to lay or down the line the house could come tumbling down. You not only know what to do but how to do it. Great! So you've just built a very well-tuned automobile in your mind that will help you travel down the road to success. Now here's the fuel—the attitude that will guide you as you travel.

The Attitude

You must live immediately. You must live deliberately. Don't walk through life mindlessly driven by habit—this is as careless as driving without paying attention. Always know what you're doing, and you'll always know where you're going. If you spend a lot of time asking yourself, "Why did I say or do that?" then you're not paying attention. Your "habit head" is running the show.

Live deliberately, with immediacy, and make your actions and decisions count. In this way you can consciously and intentionally pave the path you need to get where you want to go. Far too often we miss the exit to success because we're asleep at the wheel. Get off the hamster wheel of monotonous thinking, and blaze the path you intend for yourself. This is the only path that will get you where you want to go. Most importantly, you need to build the road yourself. Relying on someone else's standards and accepting them as your only option dooms you to a life of mediocrity. Pick your destination, build the road to get there step by step then drive with commitment and precision. The choice is yours.

This is where the power of living and thinking from your Hara comes into play. Don't live from your head or your heart—live from your Hara. Your head is the source of doubt and confusion, your heart, the house of impulsivity. But your Hara is the palace of confidence and balance, the foundation upon which your life is built. As your life is filled with those forces that increase your stability, your Hara becomes more balanced and strengthens. As it strengthens and your confidence builds, it becomes better able to support you on your journey toward your goals. Think of it: a foundation that actually becomes stronger as the building is constructed. The stronger the foundation, the higher the building can go. Live and breathe from your Hara, and ride the wave of confidence that comes out of the power of being balanced.

Now ask yourself again, "What do I want?" "What is my goal?" Name it. See it. Feel it. If it isn't real in your head, it sure as hell doesn't have a chance of being real in your life. We are more likely to believe in the things we can see and feel. This is why it is so important that our goals be as real in our minds as our own heartbeat is in our chest. But to truly live with as much power as possible, we need to be tumor free so no energy is taken away from creating what we really want.

The "No-You-Can't Rant"

You have the goal seared in your head now. But how bad do you want it? Are doubts still getting in your way? Are you subjecting yourself to the "No-you-can't rant," either from your own mind or the pessimism of others? This toxic waste dump of failure thinking that cheers for your failure with chants like, "You can't do that," "What do you want to do that for?" "Why don't you be more realistic?" or any other thought designed to rob you of your passion for success. Remember to ask yourself: Am I a victim or victor? You'd better know the answer by now. Victim thinking fuels the "No-you-can't rant." If you are writing the story of the victor, then leave these negative, defeatist passages out. No syrup in the gas tank on your road to success. So since you can't use them, lose them, then replace them.

The Can't Cure

"Can't" is a powerless word that convinces you that something is out of your grasp. Take a minute and say out loud a list of things you think you can't do, (e.g. "I can't ski," "I can't do math well," "I can't lose weight," etc). After that minute is up, go back and repeat as many of the "I can'ts" that you remember. But this time replace the word "can't" with the word "won't." Now your phrases sound like, "I won't ski," "I won't do math well" and "I won't lose weight." What's the difference between these two statements? One is cancerous and robs you of power, while the other gives you that power back. You realize that any perceived limitation you have isn't being denied you. You have simply chosen not to take the steps to get it for yourself. So "can't" no more. You clearly can do it if you choose to.

Now you're equipped to blow out the "No-you-can't rant" as easily as a hurricane blows out a candle. If doubts still remain, your desire to reach your goal must exceed the strength of your doubts. Achieving your goal has to be the most important thing in your life. I know this sounds extreme, but only this level of commitment will guarantee that you won't give up. If you want to achieve your dreams more than you want to breathe, there is nothing that can stop you.

Living from your Hara means you're living from the place within you that is committed to sustaining your life. You live successfully by eating when hungry, sleeping when tired and breathing. Now living success-fully is as much a key to your life and your growth as breathing. With this thinking, achieving less than everything you're capable of is the same as suffocating. If you want to accomplish your goals this bad, if not worse, success will soon become as easy as breathing. You are already used to breathing, now it's time to get used to succeeding. Learn to think success, talk success, breathe success, act success and live success. Before long it will become second nature.

Now you have your goal, but when it comes to goal attainment, your focus needs to be solely on the goal and its completion. Spending too much time bouncing between thoughts of either success or failure is like driving down the highway with the parking brake on. When your only consideration is success, you're driving with the pedal to the metal without the consideration of slowing down. When thoughts of doubt or failure enter, of course, it will slow you down. Eventually when your thoughts linger on notions of failure long enough, you will run yourself off the road because you lost your focus.

The Three Yous

At any moment in our lives we are at least three things: who we were, who we are and who we can become. Although we are bound by the moment and are in closest proximity to who we are, we are by no means standing still. We not only are, we are also becoming. We are never with-out the opportunity to become whatever it is we strive to be. Of course, we are not perfect the way we are; if we were then we would have noth-ing to work toward. Every success, great or small, is built on each step we take toward it. Knowing who and where you are is an important first step. So who are you? What do you stand for? What is your life for?

I can give you some guidelines to help you begin to answer these questions. You can take these or leave them, but at least consider them.

It is my belief that who you are is "now." Yes, *you* are now. You are the result of your dealings with life to this point, and at this moment. This moment you are adapting to the environment around you and changing as a result. You are in a perpetual state of adaptation, so whatever now is, so you are as well.

What do you stand for? What battles do you fight? Do you fight to maintain your ego, for justice, for what? What will winning these battles get you? I know a few people who have succumb to the hard times in their lives and are so immersed in the blackhole of victimhood that they fight to maintain this status. It becomes the meaning of their life, and their goal is to make others feel sorry for them. They are always complaining, feeling sorry for themselves and becoming outraged when others don't join them. They always argue when someone else's victimization takes center stage and the spotlight is removed from them. What will winning this battle get for them? It will get them a life of victimization, that's what. By failing to take control where they have it and not finding power through adversity, they are unable to achieve victory.

What Is Your Life For?

What is your life for? I feel you can determine this by determining where your passion and ability meet. Every person is born enabled by his or her unique composite of biological magnificence with the ability to do at least one thing extremely well. However, this one thing usually only becomes apparent when our environment provides for its unveiling. As we've found, an upbringing that is filled with "can't programming" leaves us ill-equipped to explore our potential.

However, on some level I believe that every living thing is compelled in some way to do what it is designed to do best. Plants are compelled by design to produce oxygen and some a beautiful fragrance as well. Animals are compelled by their instincts to do what they're best at in order to play their unique part in the circle of life. As human beings I believe our passion and the ability to realize that passion compel us to do what we are each designed for. What is passion?

It is the focused drive that gets a person out of a burning house. The sheer determination that compels an athlete to ignore pain until their goal is achieved. Passion is the desire for something that is so strong you feel like you couldn't live without it. For some it is writing, painting, acting, playing a sport, etc. The one thing that gives their life more meaning than anything else that they can't live without is their passion. For me it is being of service to others in order to help them discover and maximize their own greatness. If I am not being of service to others, I might as well not be living.

What is it that you are as compelled to do, as you are to continue breathing, but also have the ability to do? For me it's public speaking. I thrive on being up in front of people and communicating with them. I give to them, and they give to me. I also do this quite well. My passion and ability meet. A friend of mine is a dancer, and it's all she can talk about. It is her passion, and her passion is matched by her abilities. I'm not saying you have to be a master, but if your ability can't take you as far as your passion wants you to go, perhaps your place isn't at that level. Perhaps you need only keep refining your ability until it gets you to that level. It's your call.

I found my ability to help others recognize their own strengths could benefit those who excelled in areas I didn't. For example, I always wanted to be good at sports but soon discovered my body wasn't built for it even though my mind was. As I said, I also discovered my ability to help athletes become better. I was a student athletic trainer while in high school, and I overheard the wrestling coach talking about his star wrestler to another coach. He explained how this young man was virtually unbeatable, and the expectation this created in his mind made him very nervous before matches and threatened his ability to focus. I had been acting in plays for several years and was familiar with stage fright and had a handy way of dealing with it, so I approached the coach and told him I could help. He felt it was too daunting a task for me. I told him I could do it. He thought I was making a lofty guarantee but allowed me to have a go of it.

He sent the wrestler to me a half an hour before his next match. He told me that the crowd cheering actually made him nervous because they expected so much from him. He couldn't help but try and play out the whole wrestling match in his head to try and make sure he won, but he was nervous that he might lose. I had him lie down with his eyes closed and relax while I talked to him. I quickly revamped my anti stage fright technique. I asked him to focus on his readiness and his knowledge of his ability. He focused on this as he was feeling relaxed. I told him that the match need not be his concern until he was called to the mat. If he planned the entire match and something unexpected happened, he might not adapt quickly enough because he was thinking too much. I encouraged him to focus on what he knew and adjust to whatever happened instead of trying to predict it ahead of time. He sat up relaxed and thanked me. I followed him to the gym and watched him pace next to the bleachers; he appeared to be in deep concentration. When his name was called, he walked onto the mat. The match begun and in about twenty seconds he had pinned his opponent and won the match. I was not an athlete, but I could help make them better. When you find where your passion and ability meet, then you will find what you were put here for.

The Three Attitudes for Achievement

You may have the ability and the passion but do you have the stamina to go the distance? Whenever you plan for a trip, the issue is not whether you can complete the trip or not, the question is how are you going to do it? Any other goal is no different. Once you've decided on a goal, there are three attitudes you can adopt as you work toward accomplishing your goal. You can "Try," "Do your best" or you can "Do whatever it takes." Two of these attitudes are cancerous and deadly to your passion. One of these attitudes is the cure for the other two.

Are you ready to take action or just spend more time in preparation? Preparation with no destination is like packing for a trip to the end of your own driveway. You've got everything you need to go nowhere. Don't just talk a good game about what you intend to accomplish or sit around accumulating the knowledge required. You have to be committed to act and be prepared to go the distance. So, what attitude will guide you as you reach for your goal?

I'll tell you right now that if you "TRY" to succeed, you will fail. By definition the word "try" means "attempt" not "completion." Accomplishing a goal is about completion and nothing less. You can recognize the "try" attitude by statements to yourself like, "I'll give it a shot" or "Well, at least I tried." If this is your attitude then don't bother. You will always proceed with hesitation and doubt if you "try."

An "I'LL DO MY BEST" attitude is still insufficient because it implies that you have limits and that your best may not be enough. You are motivated by "I'll give it all I've got," when you may not know that you actually have more to give. "I hope I have it in me," reveals that you doubt as to whether you do. These attitudes contain doubt; doubt creates hesitation, decreases motivation and leads to disaster. Even if you're focused on doing your best, you're still thinking in terms of limits. Your best only allows you to accomplish the goals you currently have the skills for. If you run a marathon when you're out of shape and don't perform well, you may conclude that your best was insufficient. However, some training can raise your level of ability and suddenly your best has been kicked up a notch. Your best is always relative to your preparedness to address the task at hand. It is not a hard and fast constant by which you can measure what you are ultimately capable of.

As I stated, "I'll do my best" thinking programs you to think that if you've done your best and your efforts fail, you don't have what it takes to achieve your goals because your best wasn't good enough. This, of course, is mental doo-doo. These two attitudes leave you with easy excuses for falling short of your goal: "Well, at least I tried" or "As long as you did your best." Is this really what you're willing to settle for?

Any attitude that doesn't propel you toward success is essentially programming you to quit before you've even started. By embracing this kind of thinking, you are feeding the tumor that keeps you from realizing your full potential. One major difference between those who quit and those who succeed is that quitters always follow their own advice. They expect not to do well and when they don't they say, "I should've trusted my instincts. I told you I couldn't do it." Well, guess what? All you proved was that failure thinking leads to failure, not that you couldn't do it. People who succeed always look toward what's possible and seek out whatever and whoever can provide the guidance toward their goal.

These "try" and "best" attitudes allow us on some level to talk ourselves out of succeeding because they employ an assessment of what we perceive are our deficiencies. As we focus on what we might be lacking as an individual as we strive toward our goal, the doubt we create influences our decision whether to go for it or not. We tell ourselves, "I can't do it because..." Doing this is pointless for two reasons. First, deficits direct our focus to failure or our inabilities. Second and most important, deficits have nothing to do with our successes in life; it's our strengths that create our success. Our assumptions about our own limitations must never stand in the way of making a meaningful decision that can better our lives. Any limitation should be revealed through trial and error—not self-doubt. We must tell ourselves, "I can and will do it because..." This is the only consideration when setting goals. Our primary strength, which is the key to any success, is the strength of our own determination to succeed. The stronger it is, the further our minds get from the option of not succeeding.

Every effort for success needs to be made. Even when you repeatedly fall short, the pursuit should continue. If you find you're missing something that will get you what you aspire toward, find it out in the process, then get it and keep on going. The next attitude is all about that.

The attitude that will allow you to accomplish the goals you set for yourself is the "DO WHATEVER IT TAKES" attitude. You are guided by questions like "What do I have to do to get it done." You have taken the first and most important step toward reaching your goal. By making a Hara decision to succeed, you equip yourself with a commitment that is clear, strong and unbreakable. Your commitment must be strong enough to hold you up and support you. Resolving to do whatever it takes leaves no room for doubt because with it you are focused on taking the necessary steps and acquiring the skills that will ensure success. Any goal is attainable if the tasks required for its completion are accomplished. Your best may not include all of the necessary skills now. But the "DOING WHATEVER IT TAKES" mentality commits you to acquiring them in the process of attaining your goal. This is the most powerful cognitive chemo cure I know of.

Another profound benefit of this attitude is that its sole focus is on achieving the goal and not on yourself. You no longer think me, me, me; instead, you think success, success, success. That way the "No-you-can't rant" doesn't have a chance because the process of goal completion is no longer about you. You may think that the purpose of achieving the goal is to satisfy some personal desire. Be that as it may, you can't derive satisfaction from attaining a goal that hasn't been reached yet, so leave your satisfaction aside and concentrate on what it will take to get there. If you focus on yourself, you take your eye off the goal. If you are thinking of yourself, make sure it is only to make sure you are "DOING WHATEVER IT TAKES" to succeed.

Of course, this attitude will take work to embody and master. It isn't made any easier if you have a low tolerance for frustration. The uncontrollables of life will challenge you, like the simple things such as red lights and the more complicated like poor attitudes of people in charge or a change in your life circumstances such as health. But the important thing to remember is that these things are only obstacles if they get in your way and, even worse, if they deter you from the commitment you've made to you goal. Your progress will not always be smooth, and it may plateau from time to time, but always stay on the path toward your goal. If there is one thing I learned from the experience of cancer it's that no matter how treacherous the road ahead appears, your circumstances are never bigger than you are. If an acorn can grow to become an enormous oak tree, you can reach any goal you set for yourself no matter how big it is. Like the acorn, all you require to become everything you're capable of are the right circumstances for growth and the patience to sustain the journey. Once you establish those, it's only a matter of time.

As I was saying, doing whatever it takes means you must demonstrate patience when it's taking awhile to bare fruit and tolerance when others without vision try to discourage you. Remember that others probably won't be able to appreciate the level of commitment you have because they lack it in themselves.

Have a Day

Allow this patience to permeate your entire attitude—let it fill your day. I'm sure you're familiar with the pleasantry, "Have a nice day." It's a nice sentiment, but it isn't always good for you. It is far more advantageous to simply "Have a day." This basically means that you need to use whatever the day gives you as a learning opportunity. Having a nice day may be more pleasant and comfortable, but it isn't always as useful.

Tweaking your Hara and reminding you where you're at within yourself seems a lot more useful than sailing along with no challenges. Granted, days without incident are nice to give your nervous system a break. But learn to actively utilize those days of challenge. Just "Have a day."

Enjoy the tests of your resolve. When someone insults your ambition by saying, "You're really overdoing it," or makes any statement to lessen your resolve, use it. Whenever I come across a human speed bump like this I greet them with gratitude. For how can I learn patience without someone to test it and point out where I need to work on building my own strengths? When someone tries to discourage you, simply thank them for caring enough to be honest with you (whether this was their intention or not), because this is how you intend to use the comment. Remember, you're responsible for who you are, so you can take a negative comment and make it useful.

The more you can do this, the more firmly your feet will be planted on the track that will get you where you intend to go. As your commitment to your goal solidifies itself, it becomes more real and more valuable than the presence of any obstacle can possibly muster. Focus not on the obstacles but what's on the other side: your goal. In this way, your only consideration is finding your way through whatever is currently obstructing your path. You're like a powerful locomotive traveling cross country. You will cross over rivers, go through deserts and punch through mountains. No matter what the terrain, you have your goal, the stamina and the commitment to get there.

Remember there are no impossibilities, only varying degrees of difficulty. If you are committed to doing whatever it takes, the road will become less difficult as your commitment increases. Just remember that the moment you make a Hara decision, there is no turning back. There is only one way out: success. You must succeed, you're going to succeed, you've chosen to succeed. You're able to, you're going to, nothing else will do, because you're going to do whatever it takes.

The Failure Fallacy

Here are a few thoughts to help solidify your "Do whatever it takes" attitude. The common denominator in the shortlife span of the commitment level of the "Try" and "Do your best" attitudes is the role that the fear of failure plays.

I'm going to let you in on a little know fact: Failure doesn't exist, but quitting does. The only time your goals are not achieved is when you give up the pursuit. Legendary football coach Vince Lombardi was once quoted as saying, "We didn't lose the game, we just ran out of time." Neither he or his team ever gave up. In spite of what some others may think, they're pursuit of excellence wasn't measured by the outcome of one game because the goal was still in sight and the journey continued.

Think about it: You only fail if you lose something. Your efforts may not pay off immediately, but when your effort doesn't produce, you haven't lost anything. You're simply right back where you started. No win no lose, you're even.

Another gentleman, who is responsible for the lightbulb I'm using to see in order to write this book, is Thomas Edison. When asked how he dealt with the repeated failure in his efforts to invent the lightbulb, he said, "I never failed. I just found 10,000 ways to do it wrong." He understood that mistakes are like carving a statue: Get rid of the stuff that won't help the final product and what you're left with is exactly what you want.

The results of any effort are still results whether they were the ones you wanted or not. Their value lies in the fact that they reveal what worked and what didn't. Continue doing what worked and change what didn't and you are that much closer to achieving the results you desire. It may take 10,000 times, but if you persevere you will succeed.

Look at it as though you are an Olympic hurdler. There are plenty of hurdles placed in your way as you pursue the finish line. Every single hurdle is part of the race, and each one, when approached in the right way, can be overcome. Lombardi and Edison approached their hurdles in the right way; as a result, they reached the finish line. Like Santa and the Tooth Fairy, failure doesn't exist.

Finding the Passion within You: Coming up for Air

Now that you've been introduced to the three attitudes of success, I want to discuss one more thing about passion. As "try" and "do your best" are tripped up by the fear of failure, the "Do whatever it takes" attitude is fueled by passion. What is unfortunate is that some people can't muster up that level of commitment toward a goal. I have an exercise that can show you just how to think and feel with passion and also to train your mind to experience what absolute single-pointed focus feels like. I call it "Coming up for air." But before I teach you the exercise, I want to tell you the incident that inspired the creation of this exercise.

One evening a few years ago, my wife and I were invited to my sister's house for dinner because my father had come down to visit. My Greek brother-in-law has a way of working magic with his native cuisine, which I partake of anytime I get the opportunity. Well, one of his best side dishes is a rice concoction mixed with a whole lot of butter, which makes it very thick. As it turns out, I was eating the rice a little too fast, and when I swallowed some of it, it was so thick that it formed a ball in my throat and lodged there. I immediately began choking, but I couldn't make a sound. I took a drink, but the soda just filled my mouth because it couldn't dislodge the rice. I was trying not to make a scene because I didn't want to believe what was happening. My relatives were talking and laughing and had no idea what was going on. When I realized I was in trouble, I began pounding my throat with one hand and motioning for help with the other.

This is the ironic part: I was sitting next to my wife, who is a registered nurse and works at a hospital, and my father, who is a former deputy fire chief and emergency medical technician. When I motioned for help, neither of them moved—it was my sister on the other end of the table who acted. She got up and ran around behind my chair. She stood me up and gave a quick thrust to my abdomen. Let's just say her tablecloth was never the same after that. After I caught my breath, I asked my wife and father why they just sat there? My wife said she was shocked, and my dad said he thought I was kidding.

Either way, who did what wasn't as important as what I learned from that experience. Later that night I reflected upon what had happened and what was going through my mind as I was struggling for air. As I was sitting there fighting to breathe, I realized that I was unable to think of anything else. I was completely focused on one thing and one thing only: getting that breath. My body tensed up as my adrenaline shot up, and I became focused on that one goal. If you're familiar with the saying, "Some of the best lessons are learned the hard way," this clearly qualifies as one of them. This ability for single-minded purpose was driven into me more than ever by this incident. I began thinking about how I might be able to demonstrate and teach this level of determination toward one goal. It was difficult. I clearly couldn't invite people to choke themselves to fully appreciate this experience. But I was able to come up with something that is very close, and I'd like you to do it now.

If you have asthma, don't do this; there is an alternative I will explain to you afterward. For everyone else, read the directions, then do it. Better yet, have someone read the directions then take you through it so you'll be surprised.

Take in a deep, cleansing breath to help yourself relax, and let it out. Now as quickly as possible, I want you to take in the deepest breath you possibly can, then quickly blow it all out and, when it's all out, hold it out. Don't take a breath in no matter how bad you want to. Pay attention, and the following chain of events begin to take place. You begin to feel extreme tension in your chest and throat that begins to build and increase. You begin to feel every inch of your body focusing on achieving one goal and compelling you to act to get it. The moment you know what you want to do more than anything else, go ahead and do it. (I'm assuming you've chosen to take a breath.)

Now think about what was happening in your body and your mind. If you're like everyone else who's done the exercise, the only thought in your mind was your desire to take a breath. Your thoughts were focused on one thing, and there was a sense of urgency. You have to get that breath, and you have to act now to get it.

During that time that you couldn't breathe, you had an increased sense of focus and mental commitment that was virtually unbreakable. Imagine how powerful your determination would be if you apply this feeling to the pursuit of your goal. It would be nearly impossible to stop you. If you can recall the sense of urgency and focus that you just experienced as you thought about your desire to get that breath, I want you to do so. Now with that same focus, sense of urgency and commitment, replace the desire for that breath with a desire for achieving your goal. Even better, do the exercise again, and when you start thinking about how bad you want to breathe, replace your thoughts of your breath with thoughts of your goal. What you will be experiencing is focused, single-minded unbridled passion for whatever your mind is set on. When you proceed with this kind of energy toward your goals, what in the world can stop you?

For those of you with asthma, I recommend that the next time you have to go to the bathroom, you should hold it as long as possible. Soon you will experience the same sense of urgency and single-minded focus as is produced in the previous example.

The Double H List

I hope that at this point you are well on the road to getting out of your own way and ridding your mind of the tumors that hold you back. Now I offer you yet another exercise that will help you to cure nearly any cancerous influence in your psychological and emotional life.

I discovered early in my recovery that next to the challenging yet achievable task of successfully eliminating those toxic, cognitive cancer-causing factors in our lives that negatively impact our self-esteem is actually identifying what they are and the harm they do. Sometimes these toxic influences can be subtle, while some are more obvious, which is the case with the situation I will be discussing shortly. I created an exercise to help you identify the effects of both the subtle and the obvious attacks on your self-esteem. Actually, the creation of this exercise was spontaneous, an on the spot solution to a close friend's problem and not quite so deliberate. In either case, it does the job.

I was speaking to a good friend of mine recently when she brought up the issue of the relationship she was currently involved in with her father. Her father has been an alcoholic her entire life and, as such, has provided mostly toxicity to her development as a person. Now in her adult life, her attempts to establish boundaries between him and herself have been difficult as he preys upon her sense of family loyalty to keep her from distancing herself from him.

Her self-concept and self-esteem are continuously shaken whenever they speak. Her efforts to assert herself and achieve resolution with him for past hurts in order for their relationship to heal and grow have been met only with defensiveness and vicious verbal attacks on his part.

She called me to discuss the inner conflict she was having regarding this relationship. She was finding it difficult to picture her life without her father in it, since she'd expended so much energy on including him in it irrespective of his impact on it. The point had finally been reached where she felt it was time to begin distancing herself from him, but she was unsure how to do this since her self-image seemed to rely a lot on this ongoing battle with her father.

After further discussion on the issue, my friend realized that her greatest difficulty was not in recognizing that minimizing contact would be better for her but in determining just how much more beneficial it would be to do so. She was so used to her father's presence in her life that, in spite of the fact she wanted less of it, she was having difficulty imagining her life without it and precisely what changes could take place that would be a significant improvement over the way things currently were.

I came up with an exercise for her to do that would help her sort out precisely what she was having difficulty picturing, which was her life with her father in it as opposed to her life without him or with greatly reduced contact with him. I call this exercise the "Double H List." It is a powerful cure for the cancers others have that they wish to spread into your life as well as the cancers you nurture yourself that you just can't seem to get a handle on enough to eliminate. I will explain it from the standpoint of how I instructed my friend to use it.

I instructed her to get a piece of paper and title it **Having Dad in My Life** (you can title it according to whatever the dilemma is that you are facing). I then told her to make two columns, which will represent her two H's. You can make the front of the paper the first column and the back the second if you like. The first column is titled "HELP," the second one, "HURT." I then gave her her task. She was to find a quiet place where she wouldn't be interrupted so her mind could work without distraction. I urged her not to approach this analytically as this was sure to slow the process.

Once she was ready, she was to begin with the first column and ask herself, "How is having my dad in my life helpful to me?" She was then told to brainstorm—write whatever came to her mind without analyzing any one item and not stopping until she absolutely ran out of things. Afterward she was to take a few minutes to just sit and breathe, giving that part of the activity time to be completed.

Next she would move to column two and ask, "How is having my dad in my life hurtful to me?" She then proceeded as she did with column one. By no means should you confine your list to one sheet of paper. You may be surprised by how things you never knew were there get uncovered when you get the surface thoughts out of the way. You may end up with several pages if you really let your mind work, so be prepared with several sheets so you don't have to stop and get more paper.

When she was done with the second column and had taken a few minutes to let the listing portion of the exercise be completed, it was time to look back at what she had written. First she needed to look at which list is longer. This was the first hint as to the value this relationship holds in her life. Next she was to look at each column and look at each item. When looking at the items in the "HELP" column, she asked these questions about each item:

1) What does this benefit add to my life?

2) Is this a benefit I can do without?

3) How will my life be different without it?

4) Can I get this benefit from someone or something else?

When answering the questions about the items in the "HURT" column, she asked these questions:

1) What is it costing me to allow this influence in my life?

2) How will my life be improved by eliminating or reducing my exposure to it?

3) What steps must I take to eliminate or reduce it in my life?

4) How will this benefit my self-esteem?

This exercise proved to be very useful to help my friend externalize the issue and have a relationship with the issue instead of seeing it as a part of her self-image. She was able to objectively weigh the benefits of limiting her contact with her father with them written down in this fashion because her opposing thoughts of loyalty to her father and herself no longer had to compete for the same space in her mind.

If you were to do a "Double H List" for any issue you where struggling with, from deciding the benefits of a relationship in your life to deciding whether to change jobs or assess the outcomes of pursuing a certain goal. This one exercise can be very effective at allowing you to see the whole picture and make a more complete and informed decision about what to do to resolve the issue.

Too often competing senses of obligation and other limiting beliefs get in the way of objectively sorting things out when they all remain in your head. Think of it as a group of people all trying to get comfortable in a telephone booth, there is a lot of discomfort, aggravation and elbowing. Only after one person steps out of the booth is it easier for him or her to view the problem and give it proper perspective.

This is the same as taking the issue out of your head where it's competing for airtime with other concerns and putting it on paper separate from everything else in your head so you can give it your undivided attention.

This helped my friend achieve the perspective she needed and begin to prioritize the steps she needed to take to minimize the negative impact her father was having on her self-esteem. If it attacks your self-esteem, clearly it is cancerous. This exercise is very thorough and should provide a cure.

Here is another way you can use the "Double H List," which is more in line with what we've been discussing. Prepare your list as you did before with your "Help" and "Hurt" columns. One the top, title your list with a goal you're currently having trouble accomplishing. In the "Help" column, list the thoughts, decisions and actions that are helping your progress toward achieving your goal. Under the "Hurt" column, list all of your thoughts, decisions and actions that are working against you. This doesn't have to be completed in a single sitting because you might not be fully aware of some of your self-destructive or cancerous behaviors—or willing to admit to them. Fold up your list, and keep it with you so you'll have it when these behaviors take place.

Whenever you hear yourself saying things like, "Why do I bother" or anything self-defeating toward accomplishing your goal, write it down immediately. By doing so, your "Double H List" becomes your tool for becoming more aware of your self-defeating behavior and holding yourself accountable for it. If you can't identify it, you can't stop doing it. By holding yourself accountable for the helpful things as well as the hurtful things, you can concentrate on doing the helpful things more and the hurtful things less. This is a sure-fire way of cleaning out your toolbox so only the sharpest chisels remain.

As your "Help" list gets longer and your "Hurt" list gets shorter, you will reach your goal faster. By working on your list daily you gradually increase your self-awareness and effectiveness until you become a success machine. In a perfect world we would only engage in those beliefs and behaviors that help us. Unfortunately the human mind is full of hiccups. However, by utilizing the "Double H," you can have a lot fewer hiccups than most people.

CHAPTER SEVEN

Cures In Everyday Life

Take a deep breath, and let your brain settle a little bit. The previous chapter was a little intense, so I'm going to end the book a little more gently. Throughout this book I've highlighted the countless ways I've learned to better my life and become more successful, simply by living it and learning from everyday life experiences like a ticking clock or a bending tree. There are so many ways life teaches us, if we are watching and listening intently enough. I'd like to finish the book by pointing out a few more ways that life is our greatest teacher.

A major point I've made throughout this book is the value and inherent importance in starting where you are. You can aim high and look far when it comes to setting your goals, but you have to start here. Where you are may leave you with the feeling that you're unequipped for the task of achieving a major goal. You look ahead to the endpoint and all of the things required to get there, and you quickly assess your deficits and diffuse your enthusiasm. Face it: People don't strive for what they already have or plan a trip down the hallway of their house. You only aim for a better part of yourself and of your life; you go after what you want or need that you presently don't have. You do this by determining where you want to go and what you need to get there, in other words the tasks you must accomplish and the skills you need to acquire along the way. No successful person today popped out of his or her mother with the skills that made them successful. These skills were acquired as they pursued their goals.

I reiterate the fact that starting where you are at is the most powerful point on the road to success. Seldom do people realize just how much they can learn about success from their everyday lives. What we view as the simple or mundane tasks of living can actually be the very skills we need to succeed if we learn to identify them and apply them to other areas of our lives.

When it comes right down to it, our everyday lives are filled with one success after another. We may label them as the daily grind, routine or any other term that diminishes their value simply because the events are common. When we go from home to school or work, we've successfully completed the journey. We successfully complete our errands. We successfully complete a flight of stairs or prepare a meal. It doesn't matter the size of the accomplishment; it matters only that we acknowledge it to ourselves. We need to begin to view ourselves as successful because we are successful. The more we see it, the more we'll be it.

If you are going to make success the foundation of your thinking, then you need to recognize all of your successes, great or small. By doing so you will discover that your life is filled with so many successes that they far outweigh any failure you might encounter. When you think of it, failure that results in learning is a success as well, as long as you successfully learn what to do the next time. If you are in a race, clearly your goal is success. If you win the race, you've succeeded. If you find your stride or technique was a little off, then you've succeeded in determining what you need to work on for the next time. Either way you've succeeded.

Life is our greatest teacher when it comes to learning what it is we do well. Everything we do well can be built upon to help us do better in other areas. Our life is essentially an ongoing story with one scene connected to the next. Clearly one event can prepare us for the next.

It is amazing how many of the typical chores of everyday life, leisure, work or otherwise hold within them valuable lessons for success that often go unnoticed. Start where you are to get where you're going, even if all you're doing is shopping for groceries.

Shopping for Success

Do you realize that the skill of partializing I explained in chapter three can be learned from a trip to the grocery store? When you sit down and think about what you want to have for dinner that night or for the week, you begin to develop a clear picture in your mind of what you will need in order to achieve certain endpoints or goals, such as preparing a large dinner.

You have some clear goals in mind that you want to accomplish. What is your next logical step? You sit down and make a list of what you will need to accomplish that goal. You write down every item that you will need to pick up at the store in order to achieve the goal of preparing for the week or preparing that large meal. You are essentially partializing your trip through the grocery store. What happens if you don't know where something is in the store and you can't seem to find it no matter how hard you look? Do you give up and say, "I knew I wouldn't be able to find it. I didn't want to have that for dinner anyway." Of course you don't do that. You find someone who knows and ask him or her where it is. Wow, what a novel idea! Then you will know that for the next time you need that item.

Do you see how the ordinary can prepare you for success? All you've done here in the simple task of shopping is set your goal, assess what you will need to accomplish that goal partialize it in writing, and set out step by step to accomplish it. What we have been discussing this whole time is already present in your everyday life. But shopping isn't the only lesson in life. There are many more.

Driving Your Way to Success

I've used the driving analogy repeatedly throughout this book because it relates to something we spend a lot of time doing and thus we can easily tap into it. I want to add a little to it here. You seldom leave your home without a destination in mind, in other words, a goal. Your attitude is one of reaching your destination. Your journey can vary in length depending on the distance you must travel and the weather you must endure. As I said earlier, obstacles are only such if they get in your way. You will always encounter the unforeseeable that will cause you to have to reassess and adjust your plans. Rain, sleet or snow, if you are committed to the goal you must endure the journey.

For instance, how often do you encounter road construction you weren't aware of or an auto accident that brings traffic to a halt? Does this mean you should give up and go back home because your progress has been halted? This would be like dropping out of high school because the summer break resulted in a pause in your learning. Your progress may have been slowed but not stopped. Clearly you will either wait for traffic to move or you will find an alternate route. There are many roads that lead to the same destination, which is why on the road to success you must be prepared with as many options as possible.

Having flexibility is required for so-called normal driving conditions. Even if you are driving nonstop you are still required to make adjustments. You are continuously adjusting the steering wheel to keep the car straight. You also must adjust to the occasional pothole or any other imperfection in the road that may distract you or catch you off guard, but you regain focus and continue on your way. Even the driving habits of other drivers can demand your attention and impede your progress. But again, your end goal is your priority. It may take a while to reach it or no time at all. You need only to focus on the immediate adjustments as they are required. Stay alert for each off ramp that begins the next objective in completing your journey. Your destination is the last step, which is only reached when the previous ones are completed safely.

Try driving now with these facts in mind. It is simple to forget that our lives are filled with the knowledge and habits we need to succeed. We need only to become aware of them. In traffic this logic is a given, but it is often overlooked in other matters. Too often we are inclined to give in when we feel resistance to our ambitions. We fear we will fail or fall short, so we quit. If this were our driving attitude the car would never leave the garage. We must apply this inherent flexibility to other areas of life as well. Our everyday lives can be like our normal driving habits.

Fishing for Success

When fishing with a rod and reel, it must be done just right in order to obtain the desired results consistently. After casting your line, you must take care that the tension in the line is just right if you want to maximize your opportunity to catch a fish.

The tension in the line is akin to your level of mental alertness when it comes to spotting the opportunities that will allow you to achieve your goals. If the line has too much slack, this is the equivalent of being mentally lazy and inattentive. If the fish bites, you won't feel it in the pole and the opportunity to catch him will be missed. If you do notice movement on the line, there is so much slack that your reaction will not be fast enough; the fish will steal the bait, and the opportunity to catch it is lost. The same applies when your attention has too much slack. Since you are not alert, you are not prepared when your opportunity surfaces. When it does, you can't respond quickly enough to take advantage, and the opportunity is lost.

If the line is kept too tight, the prolonged stress on it might cause it to snap when it is tugged. Since we may become stressed as we vigilantly anticipate an opportunity, we can wear ourselves out with anxiety—just as a fishing line kept tight too long can weaken. When the fish pulls hard and we pull back, the line could break. Maintaining a high level of anticipation anxiety can only serve to wear us down and eventually break, as it is difficult to maintain such a high level of energy. The solution is to find a place between a lazy line and a tight one, a lazy mind and an anxious one.

The ideal tension is a moderate one. Cast your line and reel in enough so that the line is not straight and not so loose that it lies in the water. Release just enough so that it curves into an arch that is small enough that a simple lifting of the pole will straighten the line and snag any fish that should target your bait.

In your mind you're not aloof and lazy, nor are you anxious. You are simply awake, alert and expending enough energy to tend to what's before you. You're calmly paying attention, concentrating on the opportunities you have, so that when additional ones present themselves you're in just the right frame of mind to take advantage.

Just like in fishing, one spot on the lake may be more productive than another one. You sit patiently and persevere as you wait for the fish to bite. You may discover that either that spot has not yielded any fish, or the fish there are smaller than you desire. As in life you may have to relocate in search of the opportunity you seek. Move to a different part of the lake until you find the spot that contains your goal.

Be patient and persevere—the fish and the opportunities are there. You're line and your mind must be in the right place. When the opportunity presents itself you will be ready. Life has so many lessons to teach us, simply by going about the act of living. We need only look, listen, feel, and learn. We need only to get out of our own way. When we realize that our circumstances are not bigger than we are and when we value accomplishing our next goal as much as we value taking our next breath, then nothing can stop us. Change in our lives for the better begins the moment we change our minds.

The Seeds of Unlimited Greatness

Her is my final message, the final cure, from my heart to yours. We are born with the seeds of unlimited greatness within us. People like Martin Luther King, Jr., Mother Theresa, Gandhi; Joan of Arc, Nelson Mandela and Abraham Lincoln all understood this about themselves. What made them so special is that they knew something we've allowed ourselves to be talked out of: the fact that we are essentially great, and when we decide to live with the full expression of our greatness, we accomplish great things.

The Jews who survived the Holocaust did so in part because they knew they were great in spite of how they were being treated. The slaves survived because of the pride they found through their knowledge of their own greatness. I survived my battle with cancer and the loss of my friends who didn't want to deal with my illness. I came out a better, stronger person because I rediscovered my own greatness, which taught me that no matter how difficult my circumstances are, they are never bigger than I am because I am great. I found he ultimate cure.

The reason I know you are great is because the universe doesn't make junk. It only makes what it can use. The sun, water, food and YOU are created for a reason. The universe only makes the very best things to make this world work. That's why the universe made you. Countless people have survived horrible, painful, depressing situations, and still accomplished great things because they realized that they weren't born special, they were special just by being born. Being alive makes you great. When you realize this fact, you begin to dream great dreams, think great thoughts, do great things, and accomplish the greatest accomplishments.

The people who tell you that you're no good or that you'll never amount to anything are people who don't realize that they're great so they certainly won't see it in you. How do you think people that truly know they're great treat other people? For starters, with love, dignity, respect and encouragement, that's how. They can look at you and see your greatness as well. Always remember that no one can take your greatness away. Only you can decide not to use it. The universe created you for nothing short of greatness. When you decide to put forth the effort the time, and the confidence in your own competence, your seeds will come to life and greatness will begin to grow. No one can stop you, except yourself. So be great, it's who you are. All my love to you.

BIBLIOGRAPHY

Canfield, Jack (2000). The Self-Esteem and Peak Performance Facilitating Skills Seminar. From the workbook that accompanied this seminar (July 8-15, 2000), Santa Barbara, CA.

For more information on this seminar visit www.jackcanfield.com
Jack Canfield
Self-Esteem Seminars, Inc.
P. O. Box 30880
Santa Barbara, CA 93103
800-237-8336

About The Author

—————————V—————————

Brian R. King is a cancer survivor, Social Worker and America's # 1 Quality Living Consultant. He is also the President of Change Your Life, Inc. which specializes in developing life transformation techniques to "Help People Heal Their Future By Improving Upon Their Past." Brian is also known for his inspirational speeches as well as his rapid results one on one consulting. You can find Brian online at www.BrianRKing.com